FUNDAMENTALS OF
English
Grammar

FOURTH EDITION
WORKBOOK
Volume A

D1604632

PEARSON
Longman

Betty S. Azar
Rachel Spack Koch
Stacy A. Hagen

Fundamentals of English Grammar, Fourth Edition
Workbook, Volume A

Copyright © 2011, 2003, 1992, 1985 by Betty Schrampfer Azar
All rights reserved.

No part of this publication may be reproduced, stored in a retrieval system, or transmitted in any form or by any means, electronic, mechanical, photocopying, recording, or otherwise, without the prior permission of the publisher.

Azar Associates: Shelley Hartle, Editor, and Sue Van Etten, Manager

Pearson Education, 10 Bank Street, White Plains, NY 10606

Staff credits: The people who made up the *Fundamentals of English Grammar, Fourth Edition, Workbook* team, representing editorial, production, design, and manufacturing, are, Diane Cipollone, Dave Dickey, Christine Edmonds, Ann France, and Amy McCormick.

Text composition: S4Carlisle Publishing Services
Text font: 10.5/12 Plantin

Illustrations:
Don Martinetti: 27, 38, 53, 57, 62, 66, 77, 89, 92, 112, 121, 125, 127, 130
Chris Pavely: 4, 6, 7, 9, 11, 21, 24, 28, 30, 34, 43, 59, 79, 94, 97, 98, 104, 118, 126

Printed in the United States of America

ISBN 10: 0-13-707524-3
ISBN 13: 978-0-13-707524-9

15 2019

Contents

Chapter 5 ASKING QUESTIONS

Preface

The *Fundamentals of English Grammar Workbook* is a place for lower-intermediate and intermediate students to explore and practice English grammar on their own. It is a place where they can test and fine-tune their understanding of English structures and improve their ability to use English meaningfully and correctly. All of the exercises have been designed for independent study, but this book is also a resource for teachers who need exercise material for additional classwork, homework, testing, or individualized instruction.

The *Workbook* is keyed to the explanatory grammar charts found in *Fundamentals of English Grammar, Fourth Edition,* a classroom teaching text for English language learners, and in the accompanying *Chartbook,* a reference grammar with no exercises.

The answers to the practices can be found in the *Answer Key* in the back of the *Workbook.* Its pages are perforated so that they can be detached to make a separate booklet. However, if teachers want to use the *Workbook* as a classroom teaching text, the *Answer Key* can be removed at the beginning of the term.

Two special Workbook sections called *Phrasal Verbs* and *Preposition Combinations,* not available in the main text, are included in the Appendices. These sections provide reference charts and a variety of exercises for independent practice.

Chapter 1
Present Time

▶ **Practice 1. Interview questions and answers.**
Complete the sentences with words from the list. A word may be used more than once.

am	do	is	meet	play	you
are	from	like	✓name	write	

KUNIO: Hi. My name __is__ Kunio.
                    1

MARIA: Hi. My __name__ __is__ Maria. I __am__ glad to meet you.
                   2   3   4

KUNIO: I _____ glad to _____ you too. Where _____
                5   6   7
_____ from?
        8

MARIA: I _____ from Mexico. Where _____ _____ _____?
              9   10   11   12

KUNIO: I _____ _____ Japan.
              13   14

MARIA: Where _____ _____ living now?
                  15   16

KUNIO: On Fifth Avenue in an apartment. And you?

MARIA: I _____ living in a dorm.
              17

KUNIO: What _____ you studying?
                18

MARIA: Business. After I study English, I'm going to attend the School of Business

Administration. How about you? What _____ your major?
                                          19

KUNIO: Engineering.

MARIA: What _____ you like to do in your free time?
                20

KUNIO: I play the guitar with a group.

MARIA: Really? Where?

KUNIO: We _____ together in a friend's garage on weekends. It's fun. How about you?
              21
What _____ you do in your free time?
          22

MARIA: I like to get on the Internet.

KUNIO: Oh? What _____ you do when you're online?
                       23

MARIA: I write a blog. I _____ two or three times a week.
                          24

KUNIO: A blog! What _____ you write about on your blog?
                       25

MARIA: The news. I _____ to give my thoughts.
                     26

KUNIO: That's interesting!

MARIA: I have to _____ your full name on the board when I introduce you to the class.
                   27

How _____ _____ spell your name?
      28   29

KUNIO: My first name _____ Kunio. K-U-N-I-O. My family name _____
                        30   31

Akiwa.

MARIA: Kunio Akiwa. _____ that right?
                       32

KUNIO: Yes, it _____. And what _____ your name again?
                 33   34

MARIA: My first name _____ Maria. M-A-R-I-A. My last name _____ Lopez.
                        35   36

KUNIO: Thanks. Well, it's been nice talking to you.

MARIA: I enjoyed it too.

▶ **Practice 2. Simple present and present progressive.** (Chart 1-1)
Circle the correct verb.

1. I (*sit* / *am sitting*) at my desk right now.

2. I (*sit* / *am sitting*) at this desk every day.

3. I (*do* / *am doing*) grammar exercises every day.

4. I (*do* / *am doing*) a grammar exercise now.

5. I (*look* / *am looking*) at Sentence 5 now.

6. Now I (*write* / *am writing*) the correct completion for this sentence.

7. Henry (*sits* / *is sitting*) at his desk now.

8. He (*works* / *is working*) at his computer.

9. He (*works* / *is working*) at his computer every day.

10. He (*checks* / *is checking*) his email right now.

11. He (*checks* / *is checking*) his email 20 times a day.

12. He (*writes* / *is writing*) more than 30 emails every day.

► **Practice 3. Forms of the simple present.** (Chart 1-2)
Complete each sentence with the correct form of the verb *speak*.

Part I: STATEMENT FORMS

1. I _____*speak*_____ English.
2. They _____ English.
3. He _____ English.
4. You _____ English.
5. She _____ English.

Part II: NEGATIVE FORMS

6. I _____*do not / don't speak*_____ English.
7. They _____ English.
8. She _____ English.
9. You _____ English.
10. He _____ English.

Part III: QUESTION FORMS

11. _____*Do*_____ you _____*speak*_____ English?
12. _____ they _____ English?
13. _____ he _____ English?
14. _____ we _____ English?
15. _____ she _____ English?

► **Practice 4. Forms of the simple present tense.** (Chart 1-2)
Complete each sentence with the appropriate verb from the list. Add *-s/-es* as necessary.

collect	cook	✓play	run	work
conduct	drive	program	train	write

1. Leon is a piano player. He _____*plays*_____ the piano in a restaurant on weekends.
2. Akira is an orchestra conductor. He _____ the City Symphony Orchestra.
3. My grandparents are stamp collectors. They _____ stamps from all over the world.
4. My sister is a computer programmer. She _____ computers for a large corporation.
5. Ariel is a teacher trainer. He _____ teachers for elementary schools.
6. Fred and Ted are marathon runners. They _____ in marathon races.
7. Gino is the cook in the governor's house. He _____ for the governor's family.
8. Two of my friends are post-office workers. They _____ in the post office.
9. Alex is a truck driver. He _____ a truck up and down the interstate highways.
10. I am a travel writer. I _____ articles for a travel magazine.

► **Practice 5. The simple present tense.** (Chart 1-2)
Sentence a. is a statement with an incorrect fact. In Sentence b., write the negative of that statement, and then write the correct fact. Use the affirmative and negative forms of the verb in Sentence a.

1. a. The needle of a compass points south.

   b. No. The needle of a compass ____doesn't point____ south.

      It _____points_____ north.

2. a. February comes before January.

   b. No. February _____ before January. It _____

      after January.

3. a. It snows in warm weather.

   b. No. It _____ in warm weather. It _____ in cold

      weather.

4. a. Bananas grow in cold climates.

   b. No. Bananas _____ in cold climates. Bananas

      _____ in warm climates.

5. a. Lightning follows thunder.

   b. No. Lightning _____ thunder.

      Thunder _____ lightning.

6. a. Whales fly.

   b. No. Whales _____. Birds

      _____.

7. a. The earth revolves around the moon.

   b. No. The earth _____ around the moon.

      The moon _____ around the earth.

8. a. Butterflies turn into caterpillars.

   b. No. Butterflies _____ into caterpillars.

      Caterpillars _____ into butterflies.

► **Practice 6. The simple present tense.** (Chart 1-2)
Complete the sentences with **do, does,** or **Ø**.

1. Polly and Scott _____ not work in an office.

2. They _____ own a small construction company.

3. The company _____ not build houses.

4. The company _____ repairs houses.

5. Polly and Scott _____ not do the same work.

6. They _____ do different kinds of work.

7. Polly _____ enjoys painting, but Scott _____ not like painting.

8. He _____ prefers to fix things.

9. They _____ spend 8 to 10 hours at work on most days.

10. They _____ not work at night or on weekends.

11. _____ they plan to work together for a long time? Yes, they're married.

▶ **Practice 7. Forms of the present progressive.** (Chart 1-2)
Complete the sentences with the correct form of the verb *speak*.

Part I: STATEMENT FORMS

1. I _____*am speaking*_____ English right now.

2. They _____ English right now.

3. She _____ English right now.

4. You _____ English right now.

5. He _____ English right now.

Part II: NEGATIVE FORMS

6. I _____*am not speaking*_____ English right now.

7. They _____ English right now.

8. She _____ English right now.

9. You _____ English right now.

10. He _____ English right now.

Part III: QUESTION FORMS

11. _____*Are*_____ you _____*speaking*_____ English right now?

12. _____ he _____ English right now?

13. _____ they _____ English right now?

14. _____ we _____ English right now?

15. _____ she _____ English right now?

▶ **Practice 8. The present progressive.** (Chart 1-2)
Complete each sentence with the present progressive form of the verbs in parentheses.

I'm looking around the classroom now. My classmates are not paying attention. Sally (*look*)

_____*is looking*_____ at her watch. Ali has his head back and he (*stare*)
       1

_____ at the ceiling. Kiki and Ruth (*text*) _____
       2   3

each other. Janet (*file*) _____ her nails. Tanya and Olga (*listen*)
                                   4

_____ to something on their iPods. Spiro (*move*)
       5

_____ around in his seat. Ana (*draw*) _____ a
       6   7

picture of the professor. Dmitri (*sleep*) _____. I (*try*)
                                                   8

_____ to stay awake. The poor professor (*speak*)
       9

_____ very softly. He has a sore throat, and he (*lose*)
       10

_____ his voice. I think that he (*fall*) _____
       11   12

asleep too.

► **Practice 9. The simple present and the present progressive.** (Charts 1-1 and 1-2)
Choose the correct completions for each group.

Group 1
1. Jack _c_ .
2. Jack is ____ .
3. Jack does not ____ .

   a. working today
   b. work in an office
   c. works in a factory

Group 2
1. Nina ____ .
2. She does not ____ .
3. She is not ____ .

   a. playing tennis now
   b. play tennis on weekdays
   c. plays tennis on weekends

Group 3
1. Leah and Hank are ____ .
2. They ____ .
3. Leah ____ .

   a. chats on the computer every night
   b. chatting on their computers now
   c. chat on their computers a lot

Group 4
1. My roommate and I do not ____ .
2. He ____ .
3. I am not ____ .

   a. watches the news at 11:00 P.M.
   b. watch TV in the afternoons
   c. watching TV right now

► **Practice 10. Present verbs: questions.** (Charts 1-1 and 1-2)
Complete the questions with **Does he** or **Is he**.

1. _____Is he_____ a student?

2. _____Does he_____ have good professors?

3. _____ from Spain?

4. _____ in the classroom?

5. _____ like school?

6. _____ a math major?

7. _____ studying math?

8. _____ study every day?

9. _____ live on campus?

10. _____ do homework every night?

▶ **Practice 11. Present verbs: questions.** (Charts 1-1 and 1-2)
Complete the questions with *Does she* or *Is she*.

1. _____Is she_____ at work?

2. _____Does she_____ have a good job?

3. _____ working right now?

4. _____ sitting at her desk?

5. _____ come to the office every day?

6. _____ like her job?

7. _____ on the phone?

8. _____ in a meeting?

9. _____ work overtime often?

10. _____ working overtime now?

▶ **Practice 12. The simple present and the present progressive.** (Charts 1-1 and 1-2)
Choose the correct completion.

1. Turtles, snakes, and alligators _____ reptiles.
   a. do   b. are   c. is

2. Almost all reptiles _____ eggs.
   a. lay   b. lays   c. are laying

3. A turtle _____ eggs in the warmer months.
   a. lays   b. laying   c. is laying

4. _____ frogs reptiles?
   a. Do   b. Is   c. Are

5. No. They _____ amphibians.
   a. is   b. are   c. do

6. An amphibian _____ in water and on land.
   a. live   b. lives   c. is living

7. _____ frogs lay eggs?
   a. Do   b. Does   c. Are

8. Yes. Frogs _____ eggs in the water.
   a. lay   b. lays   c. are laying

9. Do you _____ that frog on the rock over there?
   a. see   b. sees   c. seeing

10. _____ it sleeping?
    a. Does   b. Do   c. Is

11. No, it _____ sleeping.
    a. doesn't   b. don't   c. isn't

12. It is _____ for insects to eat.
    a. look   b. looks   c. looking

► **Practice 13. Frequency adverbs.** (Chart 1-3)
Put the word in italics in its usual midsentence position. Write Ø if no word is needed.

1. *usually* Ann ____usually____ stays ____Ø____ at night.
2. *usually* Ann ____Ø____ is ____usually____ at home at night.
3. *always* Bob _____ stays _____ home in the evening.
4. *always* He _____ is _____ at his desk in the evening.
5. *usually* He _____ doesn't _____ go out in the evenings.
6. *always* But he _____ doesn't _____ study in the evenings.
7. *sometimes* He _____ watches _____ a little TV.
8. *never* He _____ stays _____ up past midnight.
9. *never* He _____ is _____ up past midnight.
10. *usually* Does _____ Ann _____ study _____ at night?
11. *always* Does _____ Bob _____ study _____ at night?
12. *always* Is _____ Bob _____ at home at night?

► **Practice 14. Frequency adverbs.** (Chart 1-3)
Put the given adverbs in their usual midsentence position. Change the verb from negative to affirmative (i.e., statement form) as necessary.

1. *Sentence:* **Jane doesn't come to class on time.**

   a. *usually* Jane ____usually doesn't come____ to class on time.
   b. *ever* Jane ____doesn't ever come____ to class on time.
   c. *seldom* Jane ____seldom comes____ to class on time.
   d. *sometimes* Jane _____ to class on time.
   e. *always* Jane _____ to class on time.
   f. *occasionally* Jane _____ to class on time.
   g. *never* Jane _____ to class on time.
   h. *hardly ever* Jane _____ to class on time.

2. *Sentence:* **Jane isn't on time for class.**

   a. *usually* Jane ____isn't usually____ on time for class.
   b. *rarely* Jane _____ on time for class.
   c. *always* Jane _____ on time for class.
   d. *frequently* Jane _____ on time for class.
   e. *never* Jane _____ on time for class.
   f. *ever* Jane _____ on time for class.
   g. *seldom* Jane _____ on time for class.

Use the given information to complete the sentences. Use a frequency adverb for each sentence.

Kim's Week	S	M	T	W	Th	F	S
1. wake up late	X	X	X	X	X	X	X
2. skip breakfast		X	X		X		
3. visit friends	X	X		X		X	X
4. be on time for class		X	X	X	X		
5. surf the Internet				X			
6. clean her room	X	X	X	X		X	X
7. do homework			X			X	
8. be in bed early							

1. Kim _____*always wakes*_____ up late.
2. She _____ breakfast.
3. She _____ friends.
4. She _____ on time for class.
5. She _____ the Internet.
6. She _____ her room.
7. She _____ homework.
8. She _____ in bed early.

Part I. Read the passage. Then circle eight more verbs in the simple present tense and one verb in the present progressive. Underline the three frequency adverbs.

Powerful Storms

Hurricanes and typhoons (are) powerful storms. They form over warm oceans. They have strong winds (at least 74 miles or 119 kilometers per hour), a huge amount of rain, low air pressure, and thunder and lightning. Scientists call the storms east of the International Date Line and north of the equator — for example, in Mexico and the United States — hurricanes. Storms west of the International Date Line and south of the equator — for example, in Indonesia and India — are typhoons.

Usually, about 100 of these tropical storms occur in the world each year. These storms travel from the ocean to the coast and on to land. On land, the wind, rain, and enormous waves often cause terrible destruction. People never like to hear the news that a hurricane or typhoon is coming.

Part II. Answer the questions according to the information in the passage. Circle "T" if the statement is true and "F" if the statement is false.

1. Hurricanes and typhoons have winds of more than 74 miles per hour. T F
2. These storms don't have rain. T F
3. There is often snow with hurricanes. T F
4. Hurricanes are bigger than typhoons. T F
5. In India and Indonesia, these big storms are typhoons. T F
6. Hurricanes and typhoons begin over land. T F
7. Hurricanes and typhoons rarely cause destruction. T F
8. People don't like to hear that a hurricane is coming. T F

▶ **Practice 17. Singular/Plural.** (Chart 1-4)
Is the final *-s* singular or a plural? Check (✓) the box.

	Singular	Plural
1. Flowers need water.		✓
2. The flower smells good.	✓	
3. Elephants live a long time.		
4. An elephant never forgets.		
5. My brother works for an airline.		
6. Pilots travel all over the world.		
7. Golfers play golf.		
8. A pianist plays the piano.		
9. The mail carrier brings the mail in the morning.		
10. The large packages arrive in the afternoon.		

▶ **Practice 18. Spelling of final *-s/es.*** (Chart 1-5)
Complete the second sentence with the correct form of the verb in **bold**.

1. I **eat** potatoes. Mary _____ rice.
2. I **get** up early. Carl _____ up late.
3. I **teach** English. Henri _____ French.
4. I **work** indoors. Mei _____ outdoors.
5. I **do** housework. My daughter _____ homework.
6. We **study** math. Paulo _____ chemistry.
7. We **pay** bills by check. Yoko _____ bills online.
8. We **have** a house. Maria _____ an apartment.

9. We **buy** magazines. Ali _____ newspapers.

10. We **go** to the supermarket. Hannah _____ to a small grocery store.

▶ Practice 19. Final *-s/-es.* (Chart 1-5)
<u>Underline</u> the verbs. Add final **-s/-es** if necessary, and change **-y** to **-i** if necessary. Do not change any other words.

1. A kangaroo <u>hop</u> ∧ . ⁵

2. Kangaroos <u>live</u> in Australia. (No change.)

3. The mother kangaroo carry her baby in a pouch. She watch the baby closely.

4. This apple taste delicious. It come from a farm near here.

5. Apples are healthy. They contain vitamins.

6. Every Sunday, my grandma bake something. Usually she cut up some apples and put them in a pie.

7. Mauricio is a mechanic. He fix cars.

8. Lili work at a fast-food restaurant. She fry chicken and serve it to customers.

9. Harry and Jenny go to an Italian restaurant every weekend. Fred go to a Japanese restaurant.

▶ Practice 20. Simple present: final *-s/-es.* (Charts 1-4 and 1-5)
Read Sam's paragraph about his typical day. Then rewrite the paragraph using **he** in place of **I**. You will need to change the verbs.

Sam's Day

I leave my apartment at 8:00 every morning. I walk to the bus stop and catch the 8:10 bus. It takes me downtown. Then I transfer to another bus, and it takes me to my part-time job. I arrive at work at 8:50. I stay until 1:00, and then I leave for school. I attend classes until 5:00. I usually study in the library and try to finish my homework. Then I go home around 8:00. I have a long day.

Sam _____*leaves*_____ his apartment at 8:00 every morning. _____*He walks*_____ to the bus stop
        1   2

and _____ the 8:10 bus. It takes him downtown. Then
        3

_____ to another bus, and it takes him to his part-time job.
        4

_____ at work at 8:50. _____ until 1:00, and then
        5   6

_____ for school. _____ classes until 5:00.
        7   8

_____ usually _____ in the library and _____ to finish
        9   10   11

his homework. Then _____ home around 8:00. _____ a
                        12   13

long day.

▶ **Practice 21. Non-action verbs.** (Chart 1-6)
Circle the letter of the correct sentence in each pair.

1. (a.) The professor wants an answer to her question.
   b. The professor is wanting an answer to her question.

2. a. A student knows the answer.
   b. A student is knowing the answer.

3. a. Look! An eagle flies overhead.
   b. Look! An eagle is flying overhead.

4. a. It's over that tree. Are you seeing it?
   b. It's over that tree. Do you see it?

5. a. I believe that Tokyo is the largest city in the world.
   b. I am believing that Tokyo is the largest city in the world.

6. a. I think that São Paulo is the largest city in the world.
   b. I am thinking that São Paulo is the largest city in the world.

7. a. What do you think about right now?
   b. What are you thinking about right now?

8. a. I need to call my family.
   b. I am needing to call my family.

9. a. This is fun. I have a good time.
   b. This is fun. I am having a good time.

10. a. I like to meet new people.
    b. I am liking to meet new people.

▶ **Practice 22. Simple present and present progressive.** (Charts 1-1 → 1-6)
Complete the sentences with the simple present or present progressive form of the verbs from the list. Use each verb only once.

belong	need	rain	✓snow	understand
drive	prefer	shine	✓take	watch

1. Look outside! It _____is snowing_____. Everything is beautiful and white.

2. My father _____takes_____ the 8:15 train into the city every weekday morning.

3. On Tuesdays and Thursdays, I walk to work for the exercise. Every Monday, Wednesday, and Friday, I _____ my car to work.

4. A: Charlie, can't you hear the telephone? Answer it!

   B: You get it. I _____ my favorite TV show. I don't want to miss anything.

5. A: What kind of tea do you like?

   B: Well, I'm drinking black tea, but I _____ green tea.

6. I'm gaining weight around my waist. These pants are too tight. I _____ a larger pair of pants.

7. Thank you for your help in algebra. Now I _____ that lesson.

8. This magazine is not mine. It _____ to Colette.

9. I see a rainbow. That's because it _____, and at the same time, the

   sun _____.

▶ **Practice 23. Simple present and present progressive.** (Charts 1-1 → 1-6)
Complete the sentences with the simple present or present progressive form of the verb.

Rosa is sitting on the train right now. She (take, not, usually) _____ *usually doesn't take* _____
                                                                              1
the train, but today her son (need) _____ her car. She (enjoy)
                                                          2
_____ the ride today. There (be) _____ so many
                  3   4
people to watch. Some people (eat) _____ breakfast. Others (drink)
                                                          5
_____ coffee and (read) _____ the newspaper. One
            6   7
woman (work) _____ on her laptop computer. Another (feed)
                              8
_____ her baby. Two teenagers (play) _____
            9   10
computer games. Rosa (know) _____ that teenagers (love)
                                            11
_____ computer games. She (have) _____ two teenage
            12   13
daughters, and they (play) _____ computer games all the time. Rosa (smile)
                                    14
_____ and (relax) _____ now. The train ride (take,
            15   16
usually) _____ longer than driving, but today it (be)
                        17
_____ a more enjoyable way for her to travel.
        18

▶ **Practice 24. Editing.** (Charts 1-1 → 1-6)
Correct the errors.

                  is
1. Don ~~does~~ not working now.

2. Florida doesn't has mountains.

3. This train always is late.

4. Does Marta usually goes to bed early?

5. Mr. Chin always come to work on time.

6. Shhh! The concert starting now.

7. The refrigerator no work.

8. Is Catherine has a car?

9. Pam and Bob are getting married. They are loving each other.

10. Anne do not understand this subject.

11. Jessica asks sometimes her parents for advice.

12. Does you do your laundry at the laundromat on the corner?

13. When the color blue mix with the color yellow, the result is green.

14. Boris frys two eggs for breakfast every morning.

15. We are studing English.

▶ **Practice 25. Present verbs: questions and short answers.** (Chart 1-7)
Complete the questions with *Do*, *Does*, *Is*, or *Are*. Then complete both the affirmative and negative short answers.

1. A: _____Are_____ you leaving now?

   B: Yes, _____I am_____. OR No, _____I'm not_____.

2. A: _____Do_____ your neighbors know that you are a police officer?

   B: Yes, _____they do_____. OR No, _____they don't_____.

3. A: _____ you follow the same routine every morning?

   B: Yes, _____. OR No, _____.

4. A: _____ Dr. Jarvis know the name of her new assistant yet?

   B: Yes, _____. OR No, _____.

5. A: _____ Paul and Beth studying the problem?

   B: Yes, _____. OR No, _____.

6. A: _____ they understand the problem?

   B: Yes, _____. OR No, _____.

7. A: _____ Mike reading the paper and watching television at the same time?

   B: Yes, _____. OR No, _____.

8. A: _____ you listening to me?

   B: Yes, _____. OR No, _____.

9. A: _____ that building safe?

   B: Yes, _____. OR No, _____.

10. A: _____ you and your co-workers get together outside of work?

    B: Yes, _____. OR No, _____.

Complete the crossword puzzle. Use the clues to find the correct words.

Across

1. Mike _____ not have a job. He is unemployed.

2. Most birds _____.

4. Shhh! The movie is _____ now.

6. Textbooks are expensive. My textbook _____ more than my shoes.

Down

1. Sam doesn't _____ to work. He walks. He doesn't own a car.

2. Kim is a pilot. He _____ all over the world.

3. Every year, the university closes for the New Year holiday. Classes _____ again early in January.

5. The baby _____ not sleeping now.

Chapter 2
Past Time

▶ **Practice 1. Simple past: questions and negatives.** (Chart 2-1)
Write the question and negative forms of the sentences.

1. It started early. _____*Did it start early?*_____   _____*It didn't start early.*_____

2. Bob arrived late. _____   _____

3. Hal was here. _____   _____

4. Dad planted roses. _____   _____

5. Mom liked the game. _____   _____

6. Kim cooked dinner. _____   _____

7. Nat played tennis. _____   _____

8. They were late. _____   _____

9. Sam invited Ann. _____   _____

10. We did our work. _____   _____

▶ **Practice 2. Simple present and simple past.** (Chapter 1 and Chart 2-1)
Complete the chart with the correct form of the missing words.

Statement	Question	Negative
1. You work every day.	_____*Do you work*_____ every day?	You don't work every day.
2. You worked yesterday.	_____ yesterday?	_____ yesterday.
3. _____ every day.	_____ every day?	She doesn't work every day.
4. She worked yesterday.	_____ yesterday?	_____ yesterday.
5. _____ every day.	Do they work every day?	_____ every day.
6. They worked yesterday.	_____ yesterday?	_____ yesterday.
7. _____ every day.	_____ every day?	He doesn't work every day.
8. He worked yesterday.	_____ yesterday?	_____ yesterday.

▶ **Practice 3. Past tense questions and answers.** (Chart 2-1)
Circle the correct verb form in Sentence A. Then write the correct verb form in Sentence B. Add *not* as necessary.

Einstein

1. A: ((Is) / Was / Did) Einstein alive today?
    B: No, he ____isn't____ .

2. A: (Was / Were / Did) he alive in the last century, the 20th century?
    B: Yes, he _____ .

3. A: (Was / Were / Did) he live in the 20th century?
    B: Yes, he _____ .

4. A: (Was / Were / Did) he a biologist?
    B: No, he _____ .

5. A: (Was / Is / Did) he very intelligent?
    B: Yes, he _____ .

6. A: (Was / Were / Did) he from Europe?
    B: Yes, _____ .

7. A: (Was / Is / Did) he a university professor?
    B: Yes, he _____ .

8. A: (Are / Was / Did) he teach?
    B: Yes, he _____ .

9. A: (Were / Is / Are) he very famous?
    B: Yes, he _____ .

10. A: (Was / Is / Did) people around the world know about him?
    B: Yes, they _____ .

▶ **Practice 4. Simple past: questions.** (Charts 2-2 and 2-3)
Write past tense questions using the *italicized* words and **Did, Was,** or **Were**.

1. *he \ study*   ____Did he study____ yesterday?
2. *he \ sick*   ____Was he sick____ yesterday?
3. *she \ sad*   _____ yesterday?
4. *they \ eat*   _____ yesterday?
5. *they \ hungry*   _____ yesterday?
6. *you \ go*   _____ yesterday?
7. *she \ understand* _____ yesterday?
8. *he \ forget*   _____ yesterday?

▶ **Practice 5. Simple past and present: questions.** (Chapter 1, Charts 2-1 → 2-3)
Complete the questions with **Did**, **Was**, **Were**, or **Are**.

1. _____ you go to a party last night?
2. _____ it fun?
3. _____ it a birthday party?
4. _____ many of your friends there?
5. _____ you meet new people?
6. _____ you have a good time?
7. _____ you stay out late?
8. _____ you tired when you got home?
9. _____ your children asleep when you got home?
10. _____ you tired today?

▶ **Practice 6. Simple past: questions.** (Charts 2-1 → 2-3)
Make a question from the *italicized* words, and give a short answer. Each list has one or two extra words. Use a capital letter to start the question.

A driver's test

1. *did, pass, you, was*

    A: _____ *Did you pass* _____ your driver's test yesterday?

    B: Yes, _____ *I did* _____ .

2. *were, did, you, be*

    A: _____ nervous?

    B: No, _____ .

3. *practiced, you, did, practice*

    A: _____ a lot before the test?

    B: Yes, _____ .

4. *did, was, the test, be*

    A: _____ difficult?

    B: No, _____ .

5. *you, did, made, make*

    A: _____ any mistakes on the test?

    B: No, _____ .

6. *was, did, the car*

    A: _____ easy to drive?

    B: Yes, _____ .

7. *put, you, did, were*

   A: _____ your new driver's license in your wallet right away?

   B: Yes, _____!

8. *go, went, you, did*

   A: _____ home right after the test?

   B: No, _____.

▶ **Practice 7. Spelling of *-ing* and *-ed* forms.** (Chart 2-2)
Complete the chart. Refer to Chart 2-2 if necessary.

End of verb	Double the consonant?	Simple form	-ing	-ed
-e	No	live race	living	lived
Two Consonants		work start		
Two Vowels + One Consonant		shout wait		
One Vowel + One Consonant		ONE-SYLLABLE VERBS: pat shop		
		TWO-SYLLABLE VERBS: STRESS ON FIRST SYLLABLE listen happen		
		TWO-SYLLABLE VERBS: STRESS ON SECOND SYLLABLE occur refer		
-y		play reply study		
-ie		die tie		

▶ **Practice 8. Spelling of *-ing* forms.** (Chart 2-2)
Add **-ing** to the verbs and write them in the correct columns.

begin	✓hit	learn	smile	take
come	hop	listen	stay	win
cut	hope	rain	study	write

Double the consonant. (*stop → stopping*)	Drop the *-e.* (*live → living*)	Just add *-ing.* (*visit → visiting*)
hitting		

▶ **Practice 9. Spelling of *-ing* forms.** (Chart 2-2)
Complete each word with one *"t"* or two *"t"s* to spell the **-ing** verb form correctly. Then write the simple form of the verb for each sentence.

Simple Form

1. I'm wai __*t*__ ing for a phone call.   1. _____*wait*_____
2. I'm pe __*tt*__ ing my dog.   2. _____*pet*_____
3. I'm bi _____ing my nails because I'm nervous.   3. _____
4. I'm si _____ing in a comfortable chair.   4. _____
5. I'm wri _____ing in my book.   5. _____
6. I'm figh _____ing the urge to have some ice cream.   6. _____
7. I'm wai _____ing to see if I'm really hungry.   7. _____
8. I'm ge _____ing up from my chair now.   8. _____
9. I'm star _____ing to walk to the refrigerator.   9. _____
10. I'm permi _____ing myself to have some ice cream.   10. _____
11. I'm lif _____ing the spoon to my mouth.   11. _____
12. I'm ea _____ing the ice cream now.   12. _____
13. I'm tas _____ing it. It tastes good.   13. _____
14. I'm also cu _____ing a piece of cake.   14. _____
15. I'm mee _____ing my sister at the airport tomorrow.   15. _____
16. She's visi _____ing me for a few days. I'll save some 16. _____
    cake and ice cream for her.

▶ **Practice 10. Spelling of *-ing* and *-ed* forms.** (Chapter 1 and Chart 2-2)
Part I. Write the present progressive (*-ing*) form of each verb. If necessary, look at the chart in Practice 7.

The Boston Marathon

A TV sportscaster is reporting from the oldest annual marathon race in the world.

Good morning, ladies and gentlemen. Our coverage of the 2009 Boston Marathon (*begin*)

_____*is beginning*_____ right now, here on Channel 5. We (*broadcast*)

　　　　　　1

_____ live from Boston. More than 20,000 men and women (*run*)

　　　　　　2

_____ in this year's marathon. Citizens of 85 countries (*compete*)

　　　　　3

_____ in the 26-mile (42-km) course and (*race*)

　　　　　4

_____ through the city of Boston. There they go . . . the race (*start*)

　　　　5

_____ now. Some of the runners (*get*) _____ off

　　　　　6　　　　　　　　　　　　　　　　　　　　　　　　　　　7

to a slow start and (*try*) _____ to save their energy, but others (*speed*)

　　　　　　　　　　　　8

_____ ahead. It (*rain, not*) _____ now, but

　　　　　9　　　　　　　　　　　　　　　　　　　　　　10

it is cold, and some of the competitors (*worry*) _____ about the strong

　　　　　　　　　　　　　　　　　　　　　　　　11

east wind.

Part II. Complete the rest of the report. Write the simple past tense form of each verb. If necessary, look at the chart in Practice 7.

Here we are at the finish line at the end of the Boston Marathon. It was a great race!

As usual, spectators all along the course (*cheer*) _____*cheered*_____ for the runners. They

　　　　　　　　　　　　　　　　　　　　　　　　　　1

(*shout*) _____ words of encouragement to them and clearly (*enjoy*)

　　　　　2

_____ the famous event.

　　　　3

What a great day for the men! Deriba Mergo from Ethiopia (*race*) _____

　　　　　　　　　　　　　　　　　　　　　　　　　　　　　　　　　　　　4

from start to finish in 2 hours, 8 minutes, and 42 seconds, and won in the men's division. He (*cross*)

_____ the finish line 50 seconds ahead of the next man.

　　5

The women's race was slower this year than it was last year. Salina Kosgei of Kenya was the winner. She (*finish*) _____ less than two seconds ahead of a runner from
6
Ethiopia. However, an unfortunate event (*occur*) _____ at the end of the race.
7
These two women (*crash*) _____ into each other, and the Ethiopian runner
8
(*need*) _____ medical attention.
9

More than 20,000 runners (*start*) _____ the race this year, and 98% of them
10
(*complete*) _____ it. Stay tuned for more news about all the exciting events that
11
(*happen*) _____ at the 2009 Boston Marathon.
12

▶ **Practice 11. Principal parts of a verb.** (Chart 2-3)
Complete the chart with the missing verb forms.

Simple Form	Simple Past	Past Participle	Present Participle
1. stop	*stopped*	stopped	stopping
2. pick		picked	picking
3.	arrived	arrived	arriving
4. cry	cried	cried	
5.	walked	walked	
6. go		gone	going
7. practice		practiced	practicing
8. refer	referred		referring
9. make		made	making
10. hop		hopped	hopping
11. hope		hoped	
12. put		put	putting
13. eat	ate	eaten	
14.	sang	sung	singing
15. listen		listened	

► **Practice 12. Spelling of irregular verbs.** (Chart 2-4)
Write the past tense of the given verbs.

Part I.

buy	b <u>o</u> <u>u</u> <u>g</u> <u>h</u> t
bring	br _ _ _ _ t
fight	f _ _ _ _ t
think	th _ _ _ _ t
teach	t _ _ _ _ t
catch	c _ _ _ _ t
find	f _ _ _ d

Part II.

swim	sw _ _
drink	dr _ _ _
sing	s _ _ _
ring	r _ _ _

Part III.

blow	bl _ _
draw	dr _ _
fly	fl _ _
grow	gr _ _
know	kn _ _
throw	thr _ _

Part IV.

break	br _ _ _
write	wr _ _ _
freeze	fr _ _ _
ride	r _ _ _
sell	s _ _ _
steal	st _ _ _

Part V.

hit	h _ _
hurt	h _ _ _
read	r _ _ _
shut	sh _ _
cost	c _ _ _
put	p _ _
quit	q _ _ _

Part VI.

pay	p _ _ d
say	s _ _ d

► **Practice 13. Common irregular verbs.** (Chart 2-4)
Complete the passages with the past tense forms of the verbs in the list. Use each verb only once. There is one extra verb in each list.

1. *be, fall, fly, spend*

Valentina Tereshkova _____ the first woman in space. In 1963, she

_____ in the spacecraft *Vostok 6* alone, with no other cosmonauts. She

_____ three days in space before she returned to earth.

2. *come, feel, lose, put, take*

Dr. Christiaan Barnard, who _____ from South Africa, performed the first

transplant of a heart from one human being to another. In 1967, he _____ out the

heart of a woman who died in an accident and _____ it into the chest of a man with

a diseased heart. The operation succeeded, but the man lived only a short time. He

_____ his life to complications from the surgery. Today, surgeons know much more

about this kind of surgery, and there are many successful heart transplants.

3. *begin,   become,   grow,   know,   sing,   wear*

Michael Jackson was a world-famous singer and dancer. He

_____ his career at age six when he

_____ and danced with his brothers in a group called

the Jackson Five. After a few years, Michael _____ a

star. People all over the world _____ him and his songs.

He dressed in a unique way, and he often _____ one

white glove in his performances. Michael died in June, 2009, at the age of 50.

▶ **Practice 14. Expressing past time: simple past.** (Charts 2-1 and 2-4).
Change the sentences to past time. Use simple past verbs and *yesterday* or *last*.

PRESENT	PAST
every day	yesterday
every morning	yesterday morning
every afternoon	yesterday afternoon
every night	last night
every week	last week
every Monday, Tuesday, etc.	last Monday, Tuesday, etc.
every month	last month
every year	last year

1. I **walk** to my office **every morning**.

   I _____*walked*_____ to my office _____*yesterday*_____ **morning**.

2. I **talk** to my parents on the phone **every week**.

   I _____*talked*_____ to my parents on the phone _____*last*_____ **week**.

3. The post office **opens** at eight o'clock **every morning**.

   The post office _____ at eight o'clock _____

   morning.

4. Mrs. Hall **goes** to the fruit market **every Monday**.

   Mrs. Hall _____ to the fruit market _____ **Monday**.

5. The company managers **meet** at nine o'clock **every Friday morning**.

   The company managers _____ at nine o'clock _____

   Friday morning.

6. I **make** my own lunch and **take** it to work with me **every morning**.

   _____ **morning**, I _____ my own lunch and

   _____ it to work with me.

7. Mr. Clark **pays** his rent on time **every month**.

   Mr. Clark _____ his rent on time _____ **month**.

8. The baby **falls** asleep at three o'clock **every afternoon**.

   _____ **afternoon**, the baby _____ asleep at three

   o'clock.

9. The last bus from downtown **leaves** at ten o'clock **every night**.

   The last bus from downtown _____ at ten o'clock

   _____ **night**.

▶ **Practice 15. Present and past negatives.** (Chapter 1, Charts 2-1 and 2-4)
   All of the sentences contain inaccurate information. Make true statements by
   (1) making a negative statement and
   (2) making an affirmative statement using accurate information.

   1. a. George flew to school yesterday.

      b. No, he _____*didn't fly*_____ to school yesterday. He _____*rode*_____ his bike.

   2. a. Lemons are sweet.

      b. No, lemons _____ sweet. They _____ sour.

   3. a. You were a baby in the year 2000.

      b. No, I _____ a baby in 2000. I _____ _____ years old

      in 2000.

   4. a. Buddha came from China.

      b. No, Buddha _____ from China. Buddha _____

      from Nepal.

   5. a. Coffee comes from cocoa beans.

      b. No, coffee _____ from cocoa beans. It _____

      from coffee beans.

   6. a. You slept outdoors last night.

      b. No, I _____ outdoors last night. I _____

      indoors.

   7. a. Ice is hot.

      b. No, ice _____ hot. It _____ cold.

   8. a. Dinosaurs disappeared a hundred years ago.

      b. No, dinosaurs _____ a hundred years ago. They

      _____ millions of years ago.

   9. a. Our bodies make Vitamin C from sunshine.

      b. No, our bodies _____ Vitamin C from sunshine. They

      _____ Vitamin D from sunshine.

Complete the chart with the correct forms of the verbs.

Every Day	Now	Yesterday
1. He **is** here every day.	He ___is___ here now.	He ___was___ here yesterday.
2. I ___think___ about you every day.	I **am thinking** about you now.	I ___thought___ about you yesterday.
3. We **play** tennis every day.	We _____ tennis now.	We _____ tennis yesterday.
4. I _____ juice every day.	I _____ juice now.	I **drank** juice yesterday.
5. He _____ every day.	He **is teaching** now.	He _____ yesterday.
6. She _____ every day.	She _____ now.	She **swam** yesterday.
7. You **sleep** late every day.	You _____ now.	You _____ late yesterday.
8. He _____ every day.	He **is reading** now.	He _____ yesterday.
9. They _____ hard every day.	They _____ hard now.	They **tried** hard yesterday.
10. We **eat** dinner every day.	We _____ dinner now.	We _____ yesterday.

▶ **Practice 17. Past progressive.** (Chart 2-6)
Complete the sentences by using the past progressive of the given verbs. Use each verb only once.

| ✓hide   look   read   sing   sit   talk   watch |

1. Jack's wife arranged a surprise birthday party for him. When Jack arrived home, several people _____were hiding_____ behind the couch or behind doors. All of the lights were out, and when Jack turned them on, everyone shouted "Surprise!"

2. The birds began to sing when the sun rose at 6:30. Dan woke up at 6:45. When Dan woke up, the birds _____.

3. I _____ a DVD last night when my best friend called.

4. While we _____ on the phone, the power went out.

5. The bus driver looked at all the passengers on her bus and noticed how quiet they were. Some people _____ newspapers or books. Most of the people _____ quietly in their seats and _____ out the windows of the bus.

▶ **Practice 18. Simple past and past progressive.** (Chart 2-6)
Complete the sentences. Use the simple past for one clause and the past progressive for the other.

Activity in Progress	Nadia	George	Bill
play soccer	break her glasses	score a goal	hurt his foot
hike	find some money	see a bear	pick up a snake
dance	trip and fall	meet his future wife	get dizzy

1. While Nadia _____was playing_____ soccer, she _____broke_____ her glasses.
2. George _____scored_____ a goal while he _____was playing_____ soccer.
3. Bill _____ his foot while he _____ soccer.
4. While Nadia _____, she _____ some money.
5. George _____ a bear while he _____.
6. Bill _____ a snake while he _____.
7. Nadia _____ and _____ while she _____.
8. While George _____, he _____ his future wife.
9. While Bill _____, he _____ dizzy.

▶ **Practice 19. Simple past and past progressive.** (Chart 2-6)
Circle the correct forms of the verbs.

1. It began to rain while Amanda and I (*were walking* / *walked*) to school this morning.
2. While I (*was washing* / *washed*) the dishes last night, I (*was dropping* / *dropped*) a plate. The plate (*was breaking* / *broke*).
3. I (*was seeing* / *saw*) Ted at the student cafeteria at lunchtime yesterday. He (*was eating* / *ate*) a sandwich and (*was talking* / *talked*) with some friends. I (*was joining* / *joined*) them.
4. Robert didn't answer the phone when Sara called. He (*was singing* / *sang*) his favorite song in the shower and (*was not hearing* / *did not hear*) the phone ring.
5. A: There was a power outage in our part of town last night. (*Were your lights going out* / *Did your lights go out*) too?
   B: Yes, they did. It was terrible! I (*was taking* / *took*) a shower when the lights went out. My wife (*was finding* / *found*) a flashlight and rescued me from the bathroom. We couldn't cook dinner, so we (*were eating* / *ate*) sandwiches instead. I tried to read some reports by candlelight, but it was too dark, so I (*was going* / *went*) to bed and (*was sleeping* / *slept*).

► **Practice 20. Simple past and past progressive.** (Chart 2-6)
For each group, choose the correct completions from Column B.

Column A

1. When the professor walked into the classroom, __d__. Conversation filled the room.

2. When the professor walked to the front of the class, ____. Then they picked up their pens to take notes.

3. While the professor was giving his lecture, ____. They wanted to remember everything he said.

4. While the professor was speaking, ____. Everyone left the room immediately.

Column B

a. the fire alarm went off

b. the students took notes

c. the students stopped talking

d. students were talking to each other

5. When it was time to board Flight 177, ____.

6. When we finally got on the plane, ____.

7. While we were flying over the ocean at night, ____.

8. When we finally landed in the morning, ____.

e. the passengers stood up quickly and took their luggage down from the overhead racks.

f. many of the passengers tried to sleep in their small airplane seats.

g. we lined up at the gate and showed the airline staff our boarding passes.

h. we sat down quickly and fastened our seat belts.

► **Practice 21. Expressing past time: using time clauses.** (Chart 2-7)
Decide what happens first and what happens second. Number the clauses "1" and "2". Then combine the clauses and write a complete sentence.

                         1   *2*

1. The fire alarm sounded. Everyone left the building.

   When _____*the fire alarm sounded, everyone left the building*_____.

2. They left the building. They stood outside in the rain.

   After _____, _____.

3. Everyone started to dance. The music began.

   As soon as _____, _____.

4. The music ended. They danced to all the songs.

   _____ until _____.

5. The fans in the stadium applauded and cheered. The soccer player scored a goal.

   When _____, _____

   _____.

6. Everyone left the stadium. The game was over.

   _____ as soon as _____.

7. I looked up her phone number. I called her.

   Before _____, _____.

8. The phone rang 10 times. I hung up.

   _____ after _____.

▶ **Practice 22. Expressing past habit: *used to.*** (Chart 2-8)
Complete the sentences. Use ***used to*** and the given information.

1. When James was young, he hated school. Now he likes it.

   James _____used to hate school_____, but now he likes it.

2. Ann was a secretary for many years, but now she owns her own business.

   Ann _____, but now she owns her own business.

3. Before Adam got married, he played tennis five times a week.

   Adam _____ five times a week.

4. When we raised our own chickens, we had fresh eggs every morning.

   We _____ every morning when we raised our own

   chickens.

5. When Ben was a child, he often crawled under his bed and put his hands over his ears when he
   heard thunder.

   Ben _____ and

   _____ when he heard thunder.

6. When I lived in my home town, I went to the beach every weekend. Now I don't go to the
   beach every weekend.

   I _____ to the beach every weekend, but now I don't.

7. Joshua has a new job. He has to wear a suit every day. When he was a student, he always wore
   jeans.

   Joshua _____ jeans every day, but now he has to wear a suit.

8. In the past, Sara hated pets. But now she has two cats, and she likes them very much.

   Sara _____ pets, but now she likes them a lot.

9. When I was young, I ate peanuts. Now I am allergic to them.

   I _____ peanuts, but now I am allergic to them.

▶ **Practice 23. Review: past verbs.** (Chapter 2)

Part I. Read the passage* about Pluto. <u>Underline</u> all the verbs that refer to the present time. Circle all the verbs that refer to the past time.

Do nine planets <u>orbit the sun</u>? Or do eight planets orbit the sun? Nine planets (used to orbit) the sun, but now only eight planets orbit the sun. How is that possible? Did one planet disappear?

A planet did not disappear. But in 2006, astronomers changed the classification of one of the planets, Pluto. Pluto is very small. The astronomers decided to call Pluto a *dwarf planet. Dwarf* means "smaller than usual."

Two years later, the astronomers reclassified Pluto again. This time they put Pluto into a different group with a new name: *plutoids.*

Before astronomers reclassified Pluto, nine planets orbited the sun. Now eight planets plus one plutoid orbit the sun.

Part II. Read the passage about Pluto again. Answer the questions according to the information in the passage. Circle "T" if the statement is true. Circle "F" if the statement is false.

1.	Pluto orbits the sun.	T	F
2.	The nine planets used to include Pluto.	T	F
3.	Pluto disappeared from the sky in 2006.	T	F
4.	Pluto received a new classification in 2006.	T	F
5.	*Dwarf* refers to something that is very large.	T	F
6.	In 2008, astronomers reclassified Pluto for the second time.	T	F
7.	Nine planets and one plutoid orbit the sun now.	T	F

▶ **Practice 24. Editing.** (Chapter 2)
Correct the verb errors.

       didn't visit
1. We ~~don't visited~~ my cousins last weekend.

2. They are walked to school yesterday.

3. I was understand all the teacher's questions yesterday.

4. Matt and I were talked on the phone when the lights went out.

5. When Flora hear the news, she didn't knew what to say.

6. David and Carol were went to Italy last month.

7. I didn't drove a car when I am a teenager.

8. Carmen no used to eat fish, but now she does.

---

*Possible new vocabulary:
   orbit = go in circles around something, revolve
   astronomer = a scientist who studies the stars and the planets
   classification = a defined class or group
   reclassified = past tense of *reclassify*: to put into a different classification or group

9. Ms. Pepper didn't died in the accident.

10. Were you seeing that red light? You didn't stopped!

11. I used to living in a big city when I was a child. Now I live in a small town.

12. Last night at about seven we were eaten a delicious pizza. Howard maked the pizza in his new oven.

13. Sally was breaking her right foot last year. After that, she hoped on her left foot for three weeks.

▶ **Practice 25. Review.** (Chapter 2)
Complete the sentences with the simple past or the past progressive form of the verbs in parentheses.

Late yesterday afternoon while I (*prepare*) ___was preparing___ dinner and my son Billy (*play*)
                                                    1
_____ with his wagon, the doorbell (*ring*) _____. The water on
          2   3
the stove (*boil*) _____, so I quickly (*turn*) _____ off the stove
                            4   5
and (*answer*) _____ the door. When I (*open*) _____ it, I (*saw*)
                      6   7
_____ a delivery man. He (*hold*) _____ a package and (*need*)
          8   9
_____ me to sign for it. At that moment, Billy (*scream*) _____. He
          10   11
cried, "Mommy, I (*fall*) _____ and (*hurt*) _____ my knee!" I (*slam*)
                                  12   13
_____ the door shut and (*run*) _____ to Billy to help him. Then I
          14   15
(*hear*) _____ the doorbell again. I remembered that the delivery man (*wait*)
                  16
_____ for me to sign for the package! I (*open*) _____ the door,
          17   18
(*take*) _____ the package, (*thank*) _____ the delivery man, and (*sign*)
                  19   20
_____ the receipt.
          21

▶ **Practice 26. Review.** (Chapter 2)
Choose the correct completion.

1. At 3:30 this afternoon, I _____ on the TV.
   a. turned   b. was turning   c. turning

2. After that, I _____ any more work.
   a. not do   b. didn't do   c. didn't

3. At 7:34 last night, we _____ dinner when the power went out.
   a. had   b. were having   c. have

4. We _____ to eat in the dark, so we lit some candles.
   a. didn't want   b. didn't wanted   c. weren't wanting

5. _____ to the meeting yesterday? What happened?
   a. Do you went   b. Did you went   c. Did you go

6. _____ Harvey told that funny joke, everyone laughed.
   a. As soon   b. Until   c. When

7. Kirk was texting on his cell phone and driving at the same time. He was not paying attention to the road _____ he was driving.
   a. after   b. while   c. until

8. _____ I heard about Kate's new baby, I phoned all her friends to tell them the good news right away.
   a. While   b. As soon as   c. Before

9. When Grandma was a child, she _____ three miles to school every day.
   a. was walking   b. used to walking   c. used to walk

10. It _____ when we left our office. The streets were all wet.
    a. rains   b. was raining   c. rain

11. After the teacher explained the grammar point clearly, all the students _____ it very well.
    a. understood   b. were understanding   c. used to understand

12. Jim _____ the keys on the table and left the room.
    a. put   b. putting   c. was putting

13. Alex _____ when I called her last night.
    a. was slept   b. sleeps   c. was sleeping

▶ **Practice 27. Word search puzzle.** (Chapter 2)
Circle the irregular past tense of these verbs in the puzzle: *bring, buy, go, grow, say, take*. The words may be horizontal, vertical, or diagonal. The first letter of each word is highlighted in gray.

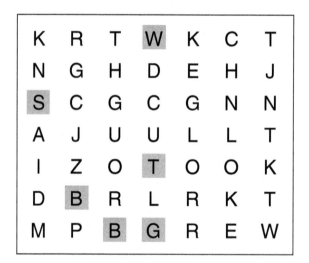

Chapter 3
Future Time

▶ **Practice 1. Expressing future time: *be going to* and *will*.** (Chart 3-1)
Check (✓) the sentences that refer to future time. <u>Underline</u> the future verb.

_____ 1. Nora is going to be an architect.

_____ 2. She's studying in Italy now.

_____ 3. She studied in England last year.

_____ 4. She will finish her classes next year.

_____ 5. She will design buildings.

_____ 6. She is looking for a job while she is in school.

_____ 7. She likes big cities.

_____ 8. She is going to live in a big city.

_____ 9. She does good work.

_____ 10. She'll be an excellent architect.

▶ **Practice 2. Forms with *be going to*.** (Charts 3-1 and 3-2)
Complete the sentences with the correct forms of ***be going to***.

1. I (*leave*) _____*am going to leave*_____ next Monday.

2. Mr. Rose (*leave*) _____ next Monday.

3. Mr. Liu (*not, leave*) _____ next Monday.

4. What about you? (*leave*) _____ you _____ next Monday?

5. Claire (*be*) _____ here next week.

6. Ole and Olga (*be*) _____ here next week.

7. I (*be, not*) _____ here next week.

8. What about Tom? (*be*) _____ he _____ here next week?

9. It (*rain*) _____ tomorrow.

10. It (*not, snow*) _____ tomorrow.

11. The sun (*not, shine*) _____ tomorrow.

12. What about next weekend? (*rain*) _____ it _____
next weekend?

▶ **Practice 3. Be going to.** (Charts 3-1 and 3-2)
Complete the sentence about each picture using the correct form of **be going to** and a verb from the list. You will not use all the verbs.

| catch | eat | fall | wake up | jump |

1. Mel

    _____

    in just one second.

2. Jane

    _____

    the ball.

3. Yoko

    _____

    into the water.

4. All the dishes

    _____

    on the floor.

▶ **Practice 4. Will and be going to.** (Charts 3-1 and 3-3)
Complete the chart with the correct forms of the verbs.

be going to

I _____*am going to*_____ leave.

You _____ leave.

Mr. Rose _____ leave.

We _____ leave.

Our parents _____ leave.

The boys (not) _____ leave.

Ann (not) _____ leave.

I (not) _____ leave.

will

I _____*will*_____ leave.

You _____ leave.

He _____ leave.

We _____ leave.

They _____ leave.

They (not) _____ leave.

She (not) _____ leave.

I (not) _____ leave.

► **Practice 5. Will.** (Chart 3-3)
Read the passage. Change all the verbs with ***be going to*** to ***will***.

A 50th Wedding Anniversary Celebration

      will
The Smiths ~~are going to~~ celebrate their 50th wedding anniversary on December 1st of this year.

Their children are planning a party for them at a local hotel. Their family and friends are going to

join them for the celebration.

 Mr. and Mrs. Smith have three children and five grandchildren. The Smiths know that two of

their children are going to be at the party, but the third child, their youngest daughter, is far away in

Africa, where she is doing medical research. They believe she is not going to come home for the

party.

 The Smiths don't know it, but their youngest daughter is going to be at the party. She is

planning to surprise them. It is going to be a wonderful surprise for them! They are going to be

very happy to see her. The whole family is going to enjoy being together for this special occasion.

► **Practice 6. Questions with *will* and *be going to*.** (Charts 3-1 and 3-3)
Use the information in *italics* to complete the questions. Write the question forms for both ***will***
and ***be going to***.

 1. Nick is thinking about *starting* an Internet company. His friends are wondering:

   Will Nick start _____ an Internet company?

   Is Nick going to start _____ an Internet company?

 2. The teacher, Mr. Jones, is thinking about *giving* a test. His students are wondering:

   _____ a test?

   _____ a test?

 3. Jacob is thinking about *quitting* his job. His co-workers are wondering:

   _____ his job?

   _____ his job?

 4. Mr. and Mrs. Kono are thinking about *adopting* a child. Their friends are wondering:

   _____ a child?

   _____ a child?

 5. The Johnsons are thinking about *moving*. Their friends are wondering:

   _____?

   _____?

 6. Dr. Johnson is thinking about *retiring*. Her patients are wondering:

   _____?

   _____?

Write the words in the list in the correct order to complete the sentence or question. Capitalize
the first letter if necessary.

1. will / be / tomorrow

   Today is Tuesday. _____*Tomorrow will be*_____ Wednesday.

2. have / we / will

   We often have tests. _____ a test tomorrow?

3. have / will / we

   No, but _____ a test next week.

4. will / be / the test

   Our tests are sometimes difficult. _____ difficult?

5. not / be / will

   No. The test _____ difficult.

6. will / I / pass

   I'm nervous. _____ the test?

7. will / pass / you

   Yes. _____ the test.

8. pass / will / not

   Jack never studies. He _____ the test.

▶ **Practice 8. Present, past, and future.** (Chapters 1 → 3)
Complete the sentences with the given verbs. For a. use the simple present. For b. use the simple
past. For c. use the future with ***be going to***, and for d. use the future with ***will***.

1. (*arrive*)   a. Joe _____*arrives*_____ on time **every day**.

                  b. Joe _____*arrived*_____ on time **yesterday**.

                  c. Joe _____*is going to arrive*_____ on time **tomorrow**.

                  d. Joe _____*will arrive*_____ on time **tomorrow**.

2. (*eat*)   a. Ann _____ breakfast **every day**.

                  b. Ann _____ breakfast **yesterday**.

                  c. Ann _____ breakfast **tomorrow**.

                  d. Ann _____ breakfast **tomorrow**.

3. (*arrive, not*) a. Mike _____ on time **every day**.

                  b. Mike _____ on time **yesterday**.

                  c. Mike _____ on time **tomorrow**.

                  d. Mike _____ on time **tomorrow**.

4. (eat)   a. _____ you _____ breakfast **every day?**

b. _____ you _____ breakfast **yesterday?**

c. _____ you _____ breakfast **tomorrow?**

d. _____ you _____ breakfast **tomorrow?**

5. (eat, not)   a. I _____ breakfast **every day.**

b. I _____ breakfast **yesterday.**

c. I _____ breakfast **tomorrow.**

d. I _____ breakfast **tomorrow.**

▶ **Practice 9. Forms with *will* and contractions.** (Chart 3-3)
Complete each passage with contractions of *will* and the correct verbs from the list above the passage.

1. *begin, enjoy, teach*

   Howard and I are going to take a painting class. I think we ____'ll enjoy____ it very much.

   It _____ next month. The teacher of the class is John Mack. He's very

   good with beginners like us. He _____ us everything we need to know.

2. *be, call*

   I can't talk on the phone right now, Tina. Our friends are coming for dinner, and

   they _____ here in half an hour. I _____ you back

   tomorrow.

3. *drive, ride, start*

   Our daughter is four years old. She _____ school in the fall. Two other

   children from our neighborhood are the same age. When school begins, they

   _____ to school together in a carpool.* The parents will drive them on

   different days. I _____ them on Mondays and Thursdays.

▶ **Practice 10. Forms with *will* and *be going to*.** (Charts 3-2 and 3-3)
Complete the conversations with *will* or *be going to*. Note: Pronouns are <u>not</u> contracted with
helping verbs in short answers. CORRECT: *Yes, I will.* INCORRECT: *Yes, I'll.*

1. A: (*you, help*) ____Will you / Are you going to help____ me tomorrow?

   B: Yes, ____I will / I am____. OR No, ____I won't / I'm not____.

2. A: (*Paul, lend*) _____ us some money?

   B: Yes, _____. OR No, _____.

3. A: (*Jane, graduate*) _____ this spring?

   B: Yes, _____. OR No, _____.

---

*carpool = a group of people who travel together to work, school, etc., in one car

4. A: *(her parents, be)* _____ at the ceremony?

   B: Yes, _____. or No, _____.

5. A: *(you, answer)* _____ your text message?

   B: Yes, _____. or No, _____.

6. A: *(Jill, text)* _____ you again tomorrow?

   B: Yes, _____. or No, _____.

▶ **Practice 11. *Will probably.*** (Chart 3-4)
Complete the sentences.

Part I. Use a pronoun + *will/won't*. Use *probably*.

1. I went to the library last night, and _____*I'll probably go*_____ there tonight too.

2. Ann didn't come to class today, and _____*she probably won't come*_____ to class tomorrow either.

3. Greg went to bed early last night, and _____ to bed early tonight too.

4. Jack didn't hand his homework in today, and _____ it in tomorrow either.

5. The students had a quiz today, and _____ one tomorrow too.

Part II. Use a pronoun + *be going to/not be going to*. Use *probably*.

6. I watched TV last night, and _____*I'm probably going to watch*_____ TV tonight too.

7. I wasn't at home last night, and _____ at home tonight either.

8. My friends didn't come over last night, and _____ over tonight either.

9. Alice didn't ride her bike to school today, and _____ it to school tomorrow either.

10. It's cold today, and _____ cold tomorrow too.

▶ **Practice 12. Certainty about the future.** (Chart 3-4)
How certain is the speaker? Check (✓) the correct box.

	100% Certain	About 90% Certain	About 50% Certain
1. You'll probably hear from our office tomorrow.		✓	
2. Al may not finish his work on time.			
3. Sue may call later.			
4. Carlos is probably going to buy a new car.			
5. Maybe Sanji is going to study architecture.			
6. You will find the key in my top drawer.			
7. Fay is going to drive to California.			
8. Roy is probably going to fail this class.			
9. Maybe Sam will be here later.			
10. The plane will probably arrive on time.			
11. The judge may not agree with you.			
12. I probably won't be here tomorrow.			

▶ **Practice 13. Certainty about the future.** (Chart 3-4)
Answer each question. Use the words in parentheses, and pay special attention to word order.

Joel and Rita's Wedding

1. A: Are Joel and Rita going to have a simple wedding? (*probably*)

   B: Yes. Joel and Rita _____*are probably going to have*_____ a simple wedding.

2. A: Are they going to invite a lot of people? (*probably not*)

   B: No. They _____ a lot of people.

3. A: Will they have the ceremony in Rita's garden? (*may*)

   Or will they have the ceremony at a place of worship? (*maybe*)

   B: They're not sure. They _____ the ceremony in Rita's

   garden. _____ they _____ it at a place of worship.

4. A: Is Rita going to rent her wedding dress? (*may*)

   B: She's trying to save money, so she's thinking about it. She _____ her

   wedding dress.

5. A: Will she decide that she wants her own wedding dress ? (*probably*)

   B: She _____ that she wants her own wedding dress.

6. A: Will Joel feel very relaxed on his wedding day? (*may not*)

   Will he be nervous? (*may*)

   B: Joel _____ very relaxed on his wedding day. He

   _____ a little nervous.

7. A: Are they going to go on a honeymoon? (*will*)

   B: Yes. They _____ on a honeymoon immediately after the wedding, but

   they haven't told anyone where they are going to go.

8. A: Will they go far away for their honeymoon? (*probably not*)

   B: They _____ far. They have only a few days before

   they need to be back at work.

▶ **Practice 14. Be going to vs. will.** (Chart 3-5)
Decide whether the sentence with **will** or be **going to** expresses a prediction, a prior plan, or a decision at the moment of speaking. Circle the correct letter.

1. The sun will rise tomorrow.
   a. prediction   b. prior plan   c. decision at the moment of speaking

2. The sun is going to rise tomorrow.
   a. prediction   b. prior plan   c. decision at the moment of speaking

3. Nobody answered the phone at Shelley's house. Well, I'll call again later this afternoon.
   a. prediction   b. prior plan   c. decision at the moment of speaking

4. We're going to see the new play. We bought tickets two months ago.
   a. prediction   b. prior plan   c. decision at the moment of speaking

5. Our team is going to win the game.
   a. prediction   b. prior plan   c. decision at the moment of speaking

6. Our team will win the game.
   a. prediction   b. prior plan   c. decision at the moment of speaking

7. You can't find your cell phone? Wait. I'll call your number.
   a. prediction   b. prior plan   c. decision at the moment of speaking

8. Uh-oh! The red light on my cell phone is flashing. This means that the battery is very low and
   that the phone is going to run out of power very soon.
   a. prediction   b. prior plan   c. decision at the moment of speaking

9. You're sick? Stay home. I'll get you anything you need.
   a. prediction   b. prior plan   c. decision at the moment of speaking

10. Jenny and I have a lunch date. We're going to meet at Gusto Café at noon.
   a. prediction   b. prior plan   c. decision at the moment of speaking

11. I'm sorry. I can't have dinner with you tonight. I'm going to help Harry with his science
   project. He's building a rocket!
   a. prediction   b. prior plan   c. decision at the moment of speaking

▶ **Practice 15. *Be going to* vs. *will.*** (Chart 3-5)

Part I. Complete each conversation with the correct form of ***be going to*** and a verb from the list. Use each verb only once.

get	move	watch	✓work

At the office

1. A: It's five o'clock. Are you leaving the office soon?
    B: No, I _'m going to work_ late tonight.

At home

2. A: It's almost 8:00. Don't you want to watch your favorite comedy on Channel 4?
    B: It's not on tonight. I _____ this movie instead.

At a party

3. A: Do you still live on Tenth Avenue?
    B: Yes, we do, but only for a few more days. We _____ on Saturday. We just bought a small house about ten miles north of the city.

Conversation between friends

4. A: I'm nervous about the flu epidemic.
    B: Me too. I _____ my flu shot this afternoon. I made an appointment with my doctor for it.

Part II. Complete each conversation with the correct form of ***will*** and a verb from the list. Use each verb only once. You may use contractions.

✓answer	ask	clean	pay

At the office

1. A: The phone's ringing.
    B: I _'ll answer_ it.

At a store

2. A: I'd like to return this jacket.
    B: We usually don't allow returns on sale items, but I _____ the manager.

At home

3. A: Oops. I just spilled my coffee.
    B: No problem. I _____ it up.

At a restaurant

4. A: Let's split the check.
    B: No, no. You paid last time. I _____ this time.

▶ **Practice 16. _Be going to_ vs. _will._** (Chart 3-5)
Complete the sentences with either **_be going to_** or **_will_.*** Use contractions.

1. SITUATION: Speaker B is planning to listen to the news at six.

   A: Why did you turn on the radio?

   B: I _'m going to_____ listen to the news at six.

2. SITUATION: Speaker B didn't have a plan to show the other person how to solve the math
   problem, but she is happy to do it.

   A: I can't figure out this math problem. Do you know how to do it?

   B: Yes. Give me your pencil. I _____ show you how to solve it.

3. SITUATION: Speaker B has made a plan. He is planning to lie down because he doesn't feel well.

   A: What's the matter?

   B: I don't feel well. I _____ lie down for a little while. If anyone calls,
   tell them I'll call them later.

   A: Okay. I hope you feel better.

4. SITUATION: Speaker B did not plan to take the other person home. He volunteers to do so only
   after the other person talks about missing his bus.

   A: Oh, no! I wasn't watching the time. I missed my bus.

   B: That's okay. I _____ give you a ride home.

   A: Hey, thanks!

5. SITUATION: Speaker B has already made her plans about what to wear. Then Speaker B
   volunteers to help.

   A: I can't figure out what to wear to the dance tonight. It's informal, isn't it?

   B: Yes. I _____ wear a pair of nice jeans.

   A: Maybe I should wear my jeans too. But I think they're dirty.

   B: I _____ wash them for you. I'm planning to do a load of laundry in a
   few minutes.

   A: Gee, thanks. That'll help me out a lot.

▶ **Practice 17. _Be going to_ vs. _will._** (Chart 3-5)
Circle the correct completion.

1. A: Anya is on the phone. She would like an appointment with you soon.
   B: Okay. Let's see. I have some time tomorrow. I (_am going to_ / _will_) see her tomorrow.
2. A: How about joining us at the concert on Friday evening?
   B: We would love to, but we can't. We (_are going to_ / _will_) fly to Florida on Friday.

---

*Usually **_be going to_** and **_will_** are interchangeable: you can use either one of them with little difference in meaning. Sometimes,
however, they are NOT interchangeable. In this exercise, only one of them is correct, not both. See Chart 3-5, p. 63, in the Student
Book.

3. A: We found this little kitten, Mom. Can we keep him?

    B: A new kitten? Well, I don't know . . .

    A: Please, Mom. He's so cute. And he needs a home.

    B: Well, okay. We (*are going to / will*) keep him.

    A: Yay, Mom!

4. A: We have two extra tickets for the Hot Stuff concert on
    Saturday night. Would you like to join us?

    B: Thanks, but we (*are going to / will*) attend that concert on Friday night. We already have
    tickets.

5. A: Why are you leaving the office so early?

    B: I (*am going to / will*) see my doctor. I've had a terrible pain in my side since yesterday.

6. A: Where are you going?

    B: I have an eye appointment. I (*am going to / will*) get new glasses.

7. A: Do you need help with those packages?

    B: Well . . .

    A: Don't worry. I (*am going to / will*) carry them for you.

▶ **Practice 18. Past and future time clauses.** (Charts 2-10 and 3-6)
<u>Underline</u> the time clauses.

1. Before Bill met Maggie, he was lonely.

2. He was an unhappy man until he met Maggie.

3. When he met Maggie, he fell in love.

4. He became a happy person after he met her.

5. After they dated for a year, he asked her to marry him.

6. As soon as Bill gets a better job, they will set a date for the wedding.

7. They will get married before they buy a house.

8. They will buy a house when they have enough money.

9. After they get married, they will live together happily.

10. They will live together happily until they die.

▶ **Practice 19. Future time clauses.** (Chart 3-6)
Combine the ideas of the two given sentences into one sentence by using a time clause. Use the
word in parentheses to introduce the time clause.

1. *First:*   I'm going to finish my homework.
    Then: I'm going to go to bed.

    (*after*)   _____After I finish_____ my homework, _____I'm going to go_____ to bed.

2. *First:*   I'll finish my homework.
    Then: I'm going to go to bed.

    (*until*)   _____I'm not going to go_____ to bed _____until I finish_____ my homework.

3. *First:*   Ann will finish her homework.
   Then: She will watch TV tonight.*

   (*before*) _____ TV tonight, _____ her

   homework.

4. *First:*   Jim will get home tonight.
   Then: He's going to read the newspaper.

   (*after*) _____ the newspaper _____

   home tonight.

5. *First:*   I'll call John tomorrow.
   Then: I'll ask him to my party.

   (*when*) _____ John tomorrow, _____ him

   to my party.

6. *First:*   Mrs. Torres will stay at her office tonight.
   Then: She will finish her report.

   (*until*) _____ at her office tonight _____

   _____ her report.

7. *First:*   I will get home tonight.
   Then: I'm going to take a hot bath.

   (*as soon as*) _____ home tonight, _____ a

   hot bath.

▶ **Practice 20. *If*-clauses.** (Chart 3-6)
Complete each sentence by using an *if*-clause with the given ideas. Use a comma if necessary.**

1. Maybe it will rain tomorrow.

   ____*If it rains tomorrow*,_____ I'm going to go to a movie.

2. Maybe it will be hot tomorrow.

   _____ I'm going to go swimming.

3. Maybe Adam will have enough time.

   Adam will finish his essay tonight _____.

4. Maybe I won't get a check tomorrow.

   _____ I'll email my parents and ask for money.

5. Perhaps I'll get a raise soon.

   We will take a nice vacation trip next summer _____.

---

*The noun usually comes before the pronoun when you combine clauses:
*After **Ann** eats dinner, **she** is going to study.*
***Ann** is going to study after **she** eats dinner.*

**Notice the punctuation in the example. A comma is used when the *if*-clause comes before the main clause. No comma is used
when the *if*-clause follows the main clause.

6. Maybe Gina won't study for her test.

_____ she'll get a bad grade.

7. Maybe I will have enough money.

I'm going to go to Hawaii for my vacation _____.

8. Maybe I won't study tonight.

_____ I probably won't pass the chemistry exam.

▶ **Practice 21. Future time clauses and *if*-clauses.** (Chart 3-6)
Circle the correct verbs. Pay attention to the words in **bold**.

Sam and I are going to leave on a road trip tomorrow. We'll pack our suitcases and put everything in the car **before** we (*go / will go*) to bed tonight. We'll leave tomorrow morning at dawn, **as soon as** the sun (*will come / comes*) up. We'll drive for a couple of hours on the interstate highway **while** we (*will talk / talk*) and (*listen / will listen*) to our favorite music. **When** we (*will see / see*) a nice rest area, we'll stop for coffee. **After** we (*walk / will walk*) around the rest area a little bit, we'll get back in the car and drive a little longer. We'll stay on that highway **until** we (*come / will come*) to Highway 44. Then we'll turn off and drive on scenic country roads. **If** Sam (*will get / gets*) tired, I'll drive. Then **when** I (*drive / will drive*), he'll probably take a little nap. We'll keep going **until** it (will *get / gets*) dark.

▶ **Practice 22. Future time clauses.** (Chart 3-6)
Choose the correct completion from Column B.

Facts:

• Water boils at 100 degrees Celsius (100° C) or 212 degrees Fahrenheit (212° F).
• Water freezes★ at 0 degrees Celsius (0° C) or 32 degrees Fahrenheit (32° F).
• Spring follows winter.

Column A	Column B
1. The plants will die from the cold if ____.	a. the temperature reaches 212° F
2. If freezing weather from the north arrives tonight, ____.	b. spring comes
3. Water boils when ____.	c. spring will come
4. When you put water in a pot and turn the stove on high, soon ____.	d. it will melt★★
5. The flowers will bloom when ____.	e. the temperature falls below 0° C
6. After this long winter finally ends, ____.	f. the water will boil
7. If you leave ice cream at room temperature, ____.	g. the temperature will fall below 0° C

★*freeze* = change from liquid to solid

★★*melt* = change from solid to liquid

Combine the given ideas into one sentence by using the word in *italics* to make an adverb clause.
Omit the words in parentheses from your new sentence. <u>Underline</u> the adverb clause.

1. *when*   a. Sue is going to buy an apartment (then).

   b. Sue is going to have enough money (first).

   _____<u>When Sue has enough money</u>_____, she is going to buy an apartment. OR

   Sue is going to buy an apartment _____<u>when she has enough money</u>_____.

2. *before*   a. I'm going to clean up my apartment (first).

   b. My friends are going to come over (later).

   _____

   _____

3. *when*   a. The storm will be over (in an hour or two).

   b. I'm going to do some errands (then).

   _____

   _____

4. *if*   a. (Maybe) you won't learn how to use a computer.

   b. (As a result), you will have trouble finding a job.

   _____

   _____

5. *as soon as*   a. Joe is going to meet us at the coffee shop.

   b. He is going to finish his report (soon).

   _____

   _____

6. *after*   a. Lesley will wash and dry the dishes.

   b. (Then) she will put them away.

   _____

   _____

7. *if*   a. They may not leave at seven.

   b. (As a result), they won't get to the theater on time.

   _____

   _____

▶ **Practice 24. Review: past and future.** (Chapter 2 and Charts 3-1 → 3-6)
Read Part I. Use the information in Part I to complete Part II with appropriate verb tenses. Use
will (not ***be going to***) for future time in Part II. Use the simple present for present time.

Part I.

Yesterday morning was an ordinary morning. I got up at 6:30. I washed my face and brushed
my teeth. Then I put on my jeans and a sweater. I went to the kitchen and turned on the electric
coffee maker.

Then I walked down my driveway to get the morning newspaper. While I was walking to get the paper, I saw a deer. It was eating the flowers in my garden. After I watched the deer for a little while, I made some noise to make the deer run away before it destroyed my flowers.

As soon as I got back to the kitchen, I poured myself a cup of coffee and opened the morning paper. While I was reading the paper, my teenage daughter came downstairs. We talked about her plans for the day. We had breakfast together, and I made a lunch for her to take to school. After we said good-bye, I finished reading the paper.

Then I went to my office. It is in my home. My office has a desk, a computer, a radio, a fax machine, a copy machine, and a lot of bookshelves. I worked all morning. While I was working, the phone rang many times. I talked to many people. At 11:30, I went to the kitchen and made a sandwich for lunch. As I said, it was an ordinary morning.

Part II.

Tomorrow morning ____*will be*____ an ordinary morning. I ___*'ll get*___ up at 6:30.
                1   2

I ___*'ll wash*___ my face and ____*brush*____ my teeth. Then I _____ probably
  3   4   5

_____ on my jeans and a sweater. I _____ to the kitchen and
           6   7

_____ the electric coffee maker.
           8

Then I _____ down my driveway to get the morning newspaper. If I
                  9

_____ a deer in my garden, I _____ it for a while and then
          10   11

_____ some noise to chase it away before it _____ my flowers.
          12   13

As soon as I _____ back to the kitchen, I _____ myself a cup of
                  14   15

coffee and _____ the morning paper. While I'm reading the paper, my teenage
          16

daughter _____ downstairs. We _____ about her plans for the day.
          17   18

We _____ breakfast together, and I _____ a lunch for her to take to
          19   20

school. After we _____ good-bye, I _____ reading the paper.
                 21   22

Then I _____ to my office. It _____ in my home. My office
               23   24

_____ a desk, a computer, a radio, a fax machine, a copy machine, and a lot of
          25

bookshelves. I _____ all morning. While I'm working, the phone
               26

_____ many times. I _____ to many people. At 11:30, I
          27   28

_____ to the kitchen and _____ a sandwich for lunch. As I said, it
          29   30

_____ an ordinary morning.
          31

▶ **Practice 25. Using *be going to* and the present progressive to express future time.** (Chart 3-7)
Rewrite the sentences with *be going to* and the present progressive.

1. I'm planning to stay home tonight.

   _____*I'm going to stay*_____ home tonight.

   _____*I'm staying*_____ home tonight.

2. They're planning to travel across the country by train this summer.

   _____ across the country by train this summer.

   _____ across the country by train this summer.

3. We're planning to get married in June.

   _____ married in June.

   _____ married in June.

4. He's planning to start graduate school next year.

   _____ graduate school next year.

   _____ graduate school next year.

5. She's planning to go to New Zealand next month.

   _____ to New Zealand next month.

   _____ to New Zealand next month.

6. My neighbors are planning to build their dream home this spring.

   _____ their dream home this spring.

   _____ their dream home this spring.

▶ **Practice 26. Using the present progressive to express future time.** (Chart 3-7)
Complete the sentences with the present progressive. Use each verb in the list only once. Note the future time expressions in **bold**.

| come | graduate | have | leave | meet | speak | take | ✓travel |

1. Kathy _____*is traveling*_____ to Caracas **next month** to attend a conference.

2. Carl _____ the office **early today**. He just made an appointment with the dentist for 3:00 P.M. He has a terrible toothache.

3. The president _____ on TV **at noon today**.

4. We _____ a party **tomorrow**. Would you like to come?

5. Amanda likes to take her two children with her on trips whenever she can, but she _____ not _____ them with her to El Paso, Texas, **next week**. It's strictly a business trip.

6. A: Your apartment is so neat! Are you expecting guests?
   B: Yes. My parents _____ **tomorrow** for a two-day visit.

7. A: Do you have any plans for lunch today?
   B: I _____ Shannon at the Shamrock Café **in an hour**. Want to join us?

8. A: Will you be at Ada and Alberto's tenth anniversary party **next Friday**?
   B: No, unfortunately. I also have a very important event on that day. I
   _____ from college, finally!

▶ **Practice 27. Using the present progressive to express future time.** (Chart 3-7)
Decide whether each sentence refers to a plan for the future or a prediction. Circle the correct letter.

1. A big storm is going to hit the coast tomorrow.
   a. a plan for the future   b. a prediction

2. We are going to leave for a safer location later today.
   a. a plan for the future   b. a prediction

3. Ralph is going to go to medical school after he graduates from college.
   a. a plan for the future   b. a prediction

4. Ralph is smart and serious. I am sure he is going to be an excellent doctor.
   a. a plan for the future   b. a prediction

5. This car is going to run out of gas very soon! The indicator is on empty.
   a. a plan for the future   b. a prediction

6. We're going to stop to buy gas at the next gas station.
   a. a plan for the future   b. a prediction

7. This little seed is going to be a large tree one day.
   a. a plan for the future   b. a prediction

8. We are going to plant vegetables in our garden tomorrow.
   a. a plan for the future   b. a prediction

▶ **Practice 28. Using the present progressive to express future time.** (Chart 3-7)
Check (✓) the correct sentence. Both sentences may be correct.

1. ___ a. It is going to snow tomorrow.
   ___ b. It is snowing tomorrow.

2. ___ a. I'm going to attend a conference in April.
   ___ b. I'm attending a conference in April.

3. ___ a. Irv is going to come for dinner tomorrow night.
   ___ b. Irv is coming for dinner tomorrow night.

4. ___ a. A new bookstore is going to open next month.
   ___ b. A new bookstore is opening next month.

5. ___ a. This old building is going to fall down pretty soon.
   ___ b. This old building is falling down pretty soon.

6. ___ a. Jackie and I are going to take her uncle out to dinner tonight.
   ___ b. Jackie and I are taking her uncle out to dinner tonight.

7. ___ a. You're going to feel better after you take that medicine.
   ___ b. You're feeling better after you take that medicine.

8. ___ a. The plane is going to leave on time.
   ___ b. The plane is leaving on time.

9. ___ a. Take an umbrella. If you don't, you're going to get wet.
   ___ b. Take an umbrella. If you don't, you're getting wet.

10. ___ a. I ordered a new computer. It's going to arrive next week.
    ___ b. I ordered a new computer. It's arriving next week.

▶ **Practice 29. Using the simple present to express future time.** (Chart 3-8)
Complete each sentence with one of the verbs in the list. Use the simple present to express future time.

arrive	close	end	get in	open
begin	depart	finish	leave	start

1. A: What time ___*does*___ class ___*begin / start*___ tomorrow morning?

   B: It ___*begins / starts*___ at eight o'clock sharp.

2. A: The coffee shop _____ at seven o'clock tomorrow morning. I'll meet you there at 7:15.

   B: Okay. I'll be there.

3. A: What time are you going to go to the airport tonight?

   B: Tom's plane _____ around 7:15, but I think I'll go a little early in case it gets in ahead of schedule.

4. A: What's the hurry?

   B: I've got to take a shower, change clothes, and get to the stadium fast. The game _____ in forty-five minutes, and I don't want to miss the beginning.

5. A: What time _____ the dry cleaners _____ this evening? If I don't get there in time, I'll have nothing to wear to the party tonight.

   B: It _____ at 6:00. I can pick up your dry cleaning for you.

   A: Hey, thanks! That'll really help!

6. A: What time should we go to the theater tomorrow night?

   B: The doors _____ at 6:00 P.M., but we don't need to be there that early. The show _____ at 8:00. If we _____ at the theater by 7:15, we'll be there in plenty of time. The show _____ around 10:30, so we can be back home by a little after 11:00.

7. A: I've enjoyed my visit with you, but tomorrow I have to go back home.

   B: What time _____ your flight _____ tomorrow?

   A: It _____ at 12:34 P.M. I want to be at the airport an hour early, so we should leave here around 10:30, if that's okay with you.

B: Sure. What time _____ your flight _____ in Mexico City?

A: It's about a three-hour flight. I'll get in around 4:30 Mexico City time.

▶ **Practice 30. Using *be about to.*** (Chart 3-9)
Write the letter in Column B that correctly answers the question in Column A.

What does it usually mean if . . .

Column A

1. the sky is very gray and cloudy? ____

2. Jack is leaving his house with his keys in his hand? ____

3. the teacher is picking up a piece of chalk? ____

4. it is 6:59 A.M. and your alarm clock is set for 7:00 A.M.? ____

5. it is 7:58 P.M. and the president is going to give a speech at 8:00 P.M.? ____

6. Tim is holding a fork in his hand and looking at a plate of warm pasta? ____

7. Bob is standing up inside a canoe? ____

8. the plane is slowly coming toward the runway and its wheels are down? ____

Column B

a. It means that he is about to write on the blackboard.

b. It means that he is about to speak.

c. It means that he is about to eat.

d. It means that it is about to rain.

e. It means that it is about to land.

f. It means that he is about to get into his car.

g. It means that he is about to fall out.

h. It means that it is about to ring.

▶ **Practice 31. Parallel verbs.** (Chart 3-10)
Complete the sentences with the correct form of the verbs in parentheses.

1. My classmates are going to meet at Danny's and (*study*) _____study_____ together tonight.

2. Tomorrow the sun will rise at 6:34 and (*set*) _____ at 8:59.

3. Last night, I was listening to music and (*do*) _____ my homework when Kim stopped by.

4. Next weekend, Nick is going to meet his friends downtown and (*go*) _____ to a soccer game.

5. My pen slipped out of my hand and (*fall*) _____ to the floor.

6. Alex is at his computer. He (*write*) _____ emails and (*wait*) _____ for responses.

7. Every morning without exception, Mrs. Carter (*take*) _____ her dog for a walk and (*buy*) _____ a newspaper at Charlie's newsstand.

8. Before I (*go*) _____ to your boss and (*tell*) _____ her about your mistake, I want to give you an opportunity to explain it to her yourself.

9. Next month, I (*take*) _____ my vacation and (*forget*) _____ about everything that is connected to my job.

10. Kathy thinks I was the cause of her problems, but I wasn't. Someday she (*discover*) _____ the truth and (*apologize*) _____ to me.

▶ **Practice 32. Editing.** (Chapter 3)
Correct the errors.

1. My friends will to join us after work.

2. Maybe the party ends soon.

3. On Friday, our school close early so teachers can go to a workshop.

4. It's raining tomorrow.

5. Our company is going to sells computer equipment to schools.

6. Give Grandpa a hug. He's about to leaving.

7. Mr. Scott is going to retire and moving to a warmer climate.

8. If your soccer team will win the championship tomorrow, we'll have a big celebration for you.

9. I bought this cloth because I will make some curtains for my bedroom.

10. I moving to London when I will finish my education here.

11. Are you going go to the meeting?

12. I opened the door and walk to the front of the room.

13. When will you going to move into your new apartment?

14. Maybe I celebrate my 30th birthday with my friends at a restaurant.

▶ **Practice 33. Verb tense review.** (Chapters 1 → 3)
Complete the sentences with the correct form of the verb in parentheses.

Part I.

Right now it's almost midnight. I'm still at my computer. I (*work*) _____*am working*_____ late
₁
tonight because I (*need*) _____ to finish this report before tomorrow. Before I
₂
(*go*) _____ to bed tonight, I (*finish*) _____ the report and
₃ ₄
(*write*) _____ a couple of emails too.
₅

Part II.

I (*stay*) _____ up very late last night too. While I (*read*) _____ a
₆ ₇
book, I (*hear*) _____ a noise outside. When I (*go*) _____ outside to
₈ ₉
find out about the noise, I (*see, not*) _____ anything in the dark. But when I
₁₀
(*go*) _____ outside early this morning, I (*find*) _____ garbage all
₁₁ ₁₂
over my lawn. A bear from the woods probably (*make*) _____ the mess.
₁₃

Part III.

Jack (*watch*) _____ a football game on TV right now. He
    14
(*watch, always*) _____ football on Sunday afternoons. As soon as the
    15
game (*be*) _____ over, he (*mow*) _____ the grass in the back yard.
    16   17

Part IV.

It's cold today. Right now I (*make*) _____ potato soup . It (*cook*)
    18
_____ on the stove. I remember potato soup from my childhood days. When
    19
we (*be*) _____ children, my mother (*make, used to*) _____ potato soup for
    20   21
us when the weather (*get*) _____ cold.
    22

Part V.

We (*go*) _____ to New York next week. When we (*be*) _____ in New
    23   24
York next week, we (*see*) _____ a couple of plays on Broadway. Last week we
    25
(*buy*) _____ tickets online for two plays. We (*buy, always*)
    26
_____ the tickets online before we (*leave*) _____ on a trip. We
    27   28
(*stay, usually*) _____ at a small hotel near the theater district.
    29
But, when we (*be*) _____ in New York next week, we (*stay, not*)
    30
_____ at that hotel. When we (*try*) _____ to make reservations
    31   32
last week, the hotel (*be*) _____ full. We (*stay, may*) _____ with friends
    33   34
in the city, or maybe we (*stay*) _____ with our cousins in the suburbs.
    35

Part VI.

Mark is obsessed with video games. He (*play*) _____ video games morning, noon,
    36
and night. Sometimes he (*skip*) _____ class to play them. Right now he (*do, not*)
    37
_____ very well in school. If he (*study, not*) _____ harder
    38   39

and (*go*) _____ to class every day, he (*flunk*) _____ out of
                    40   41
school.

Part VII.

I had a dream last night. In the dream, I (*see*) _____ the man who stole the radio from my
                                                      42
car last Friday. I (*run*) _____ after him, (*catch*) _____ him, and (*knock*)
                            43   44
_____ him down. A passerby (*call*) _____ the police on her cell
          45   46
phone. I sat on the man while I (*wait*) _____ for them to come. After the police (*get*)
                                          47
_____ there and (*understand*) _____ the situation, they (*put*)
      48   49
_____ handcuffs on him and (*take*) _____ him to jail. Then the dream
      50   51
(*end*) _____ and I (*wake*) _____ up.
                  52   53

▶ **Practice 34. Crossword puzzle.**
Complete the puzzle. Use the clues to find the correct words.

Across

  3. We won't go to the beach if it _____.

  7. We'll call you as soon as we _____ at the airport.

  8. _____ I will pass this course. I just don't know!

Down

  1. Carl _____ won't get the job. He really doesn't have the right skills for it.

  2. If Ted needs a ride, tell him that I _____ pick him up at 6:30.

  4. Maria is going to have a cup of coffee before she _____ work.

  5. The schools are _____ to be closed on Monday because it's a holiday.

  6. Please turn off your cell phones. The concert is about to _____.

  8. Helen _____ come to the movie with us. She's not sure.

Chapter 4
Present Perfect and Past Perfect

▶ **Practice 1. Past participles.** (Chart 4-1)
Circle the past participle in each group.

1.	finish	(finished)	finishing
2.	stopped	stopping	stops
3.	puts	put	putting
4.	knew	knowing	known
5.	be	been	were
6.	wanting	wanted	wants
7.	saying	said	say
8.	having	have	had
9.	gone	go	went
10.	took	taken	taking

▶ **Practice 2. Review: irregular verbs.** (Charts 2-4, 2-5, and 4-1)
Write each verb in the correct group.

bring	feed	keep	quit	sink	teach
buy	fight	let	✓ring	sit	think
catch	find	meet	set	stand	upset
cut	have	pay	shut	stick	weep
drink	✓hurt	put	sing	swim	✓win

Group I. Simple form, simple past, and past participle are the same.

Simple Form	Simple Past	Past Participle	Simple Form	Simple Past	Past Participle
hurt	_hurt_	_hurt_	_____	_____	_____
_____	_____	_____	_____	_____	_____
_____	_____	_____	_____	_____	_____
_____	_____	_____	_____	_____	_____

Group II. The vowel changes: i → a → u.

Simple Form	Simple Past	Past Participle
ring	rang	rung

Group III. Simple past and past participle are the same.

Simple Form	Simple Past	Past Participle
win	won	won

▶ **Practice 3. Present perfect with *since* and *for.*** (Chart 4-2)
Complete the sentence with the present perfect form of the verb in the first sentence.

1. Mr. Woods **teaches** chemistry at Central High School. He _____ there for 17 years.

2. Marvin **sells** cars. He began selling cars in 2000. Marvin _____ cars since 2000.

3. John **loves** Mary. He _____ her since they were teenagers.

4. I **have** a pain in my side. I _____ this pain for about two weeks.

5. You **know** my cousin Rita, don't you? You _____ her since you were in college, right?

6. Clara and Tom are going to **play** tennis on Saturday morning. They _____ tennis together on Saturday mornings for years.

7. I am going to **get up** early again tomorrow so that I can do my exercises. I _____ up early for the past month, and I have exercised every day.

8. My cousins **go** to their house in the mountains every summer. They
_____ to their summer home ever since I can remember.

9. Alaska and Hawaii **are** the newest states of the United States. They became states in 1950.
They _____ states for more than 50 years.

10. Brazil **is** an independent country. Brazil _____ an independent
country since 1822.

▶ **Practice 4. Present perfect with *since* and *for*.** (Chart 4-2)
Complete the sentences with *since* or *for*.

1. David has worked for the power company _____*since*_____ 1999.

2. His brother has worked for the power company _____*for*_____ five years.

3. I have known Peter Gowan _____ September.

4. I've known his sister _____ three months.

5. Jonas has been in a wheelchair _____ a year.

6. He's had a bad back _____ he was in a car accident.

7. My vision has improved _____ I got new reading glasses.

8. I've had a toothache _____ yesterday morning.

9. The shoe store on the corner has been there _____ 1920.

10. It has been there _____ almost a hundred years.

▶ **Practice 5. Present perfect with *since* and *for*.** (Chart 4-2)
Rewrite the sentences using *since* or *for*.

1. I was in this class a month ago, and I am in this class now.
I have been in this class for a month.

2. I knew my teacher in September, and I know her now.

3. Sam wanted a dog two years ago, and he wants one now.

4. Sara needed a new car last year, and she still needs one.

5. Our professor was sick a week ago, and she is still sick.

6. My parents live in Canada. They moved there in December.

7. I know Mrs. Brown. I met her in 1999.

8. Tom works at a fast-food restaurant. He got the job three weeks ago.

▶ **Practice 6. Negative, question, and short-answer forms.** (Chart 4-3)
Complete the conversations with the given verbs and any words in parentheses. Use the present
perfect.

1. *eat* A: (*you, ever*) _____*Have you ever eaten*_____ pepperoni pizza?
B: Yes, I _____*have*_____. I _____*have eaten*_____ pepperoni pizza many
times. OR
No, I _____*haven't*_____. I (*never*) _____*have never eaten*_____
pepperoni pizza.

2. *talk* A: (*you, ever*) _____ to a famous person?

B: Yes, I _____. I _____ to a lot of famous people.

OR

No, I _____. I (*never*) _____ to a famous person.

3. *rent* A: (*Erica, ever*) _____ a car?

B: Yes, she _____. She _____ a car many times.

OR

No, she _____. She (*never*) _____ a car.

4. *see* A: (*you, ever*) _____ a shooting star?

B: Yes, I _____. I _____ a lot of shooting stars.

OR

No, I _____. I (*never*) _____ a shooting star.

5. *catch* A: (*Joe, ever*) _____ a big fish?

B: Yes, he _____. He _____ lots of big fish. OR

No, he _____. He (*never*) _____ a big fish.

6. *have* A: (*you, ever*) _____ a bad sunburn?

B: Yes, I _____. I _____ a bad sunburn several times. OR

No, I _____. I (*never*) _____ a bad sunburn.

7. *meet* A: (*I, ever*) _____ you before?

B: Yes, you _____. You _____ me before. OR

No, you _____. You (*never*) _____ me before.

8. *be* A: (*the boys, ever*) _____ to a baseball game before?

B: Yes, they _____. They _____ to a few baseball games. OR

No, they _____. They (*never*) _____ to a baseball game.

▶ **Practice 7. Negative, question, and short-answer forms.** (Charts 4-3 and 4-4)
Complete the questions and statements with the given verbs and any words in parentheses.

A TV Interview with a Famous Actress

BRYAN: Welcome to our show, Ms. Starr.

LARA: Thank you. I'm glad to be here. By the way, please call me Lara.

BRYAN: Okay, Lara. Well, first, how long (*be*) ___*have you been*___ in movies?
                                                                     1

LARA: For many years — since I was a teenager.

BRYAN: Really? How many movies (*make, you*) _____ so far?
                                                                              2

LARA: I've made about twenty movies.

BRYAN: (*enjoy, you, always*) _____ your work,
                                                              3

ever since you began in your teens?

LARA: Yes, I _____. I have always loved my work.
                      4

BRYAN: Lara, you travel a lot in your work, right?

LARA: Oh, yes. I travel very often.

BRYAN: Where (*travel, you*) _____ to so far?

 ₅

LARA: I (*be*) _____ to Europe, Africa, and Asia for my work.

 ₆

BRYAN: Do you miss your friends and family when you are away? Have you ever wanted a more

normal life?

LARA: Well, I miss my friends and family, but I (*never, want*)

_____ a regular life. I've always been very happy in

 ₇

my work.

BRYAN: (*think, you, ever*) _____ about getting married?

 ₈

LARA: Well, no, I _____. Maybe that's because I (*not, meet*)

 ₉

_____ any really nice guys recently. Maybe I will meet

 ₁₀

someone nice, and maybe I won't. Either way, it's okay with me.

▶ **Practice 8. Present perfect with unspecified time.** (Chart 4-4)
Choose the correct completions. Both answers may be correct.

1. The year hasn't ended _____. There is still time to pay your taxes before December 30th.
   a. already   b. yet

2. Winter arrived early this year. It has snowed twice _____, and summer isn't even over!
   a. already   b. yet

3. Have you finished your homework _____?
   a. already   b. yet

4. Kate has _____ returned from a year in Tokyo.
   a. already   b. yet

5. I'm not quite ready to leave. I haven't finished packing my suitcase _____.
   a. already   b. yet

6. Have you seen the new Indian movie _____?
   a. already   b. yet

7. Malcolm doesn't need to take another science course. He has
   _____ taken the required number of science classes.
   a. already   b. yet

8. Since he retired, our neighbor Mr. Evans has _____ gained about
   30 pounds. That's because he just sits in front of the TV all day.
   He has become a real couch potato!*
   a. already   b. yet

---

*couch potato= an informal phrase to describe someone who spends a lot of time sitting or lying down and watching television

Complete the sentences with the words in the list. There is one extra word in each list.

1. *has, school, started, not, yet, already*

   Our daughter is only two years old, so she _____ *has not started school yet.* _____

   She is too young.

2. *has, learned, already, yet, the alphabet*

   Our daughter is only two years old, but she _____

   _____. Isn't she smart?

3. *already, corrected, has, yet, our tests*

   Our teacher works very quickly. She _____

   _____. She corrected them all in one hour!

4. *returned, the tests, not, has, already, yet*

   Our teacher corrected the tests last night, but she left them at home. She _____

   _____. I guess that she will return

   them tomorrow.

5. *not, already, yet, dinner, cooked, has*

   Anita _____ because she came home

   late from her job.

6. *cooked, already, yet, has, dinner*

   Anita _____. She got home early and she wants

   to go to bed early.

▶ Practice 10. Present perfect with unspecified time. (Chart 4-4)
Complete each sentence with a verb from the list. Include any words that are in parentheses. Use the present perfect form of the verb. Use a negative form if appropriate.

change	invite	✓meet	retire	spend
give	live	pick	see	travel

Neighbors in My Apartment Building

A few months ago, I moved to a new apartment. I (*all my neighbors / yet*)

_____ *haven't met all my neighbors yet* _____, but I have met some of them. They are

₁

interesting people.

My neighbor in 3G is a private pilot. Last week he returned from the South Pole, and before that

he was in Africa. He _____ all over the world.

₂

My neighbor in 4F is a doctor, but she looks like a punk rocker*. She (*already*)

_____ the color of her hair four or five times since I moved in.
₃

Now it's purple.

The young man across the hall has a lot of parties. He (*already*)

_____ several parties since I moved in, but he (*not*)
₄

_____ me to any of them.
₅

My next-door neighbors are musicians. They (*just*) _____ from
₆

the City Symphony Orchestra. They were with the orchestra for more than 20 years. Now they are

looking forward to traveling and spending more time with their family.

The neighbors on the other side are mysterious. I saw them only once, but I (*not*)

_____ them for a while. Nobody has. They (*not*)
₇

_____ up their newspapers for a week. There are six or seven newspapers
₈

on the floor in front of their door.

A young woman in the building is my new best friend. She _____ here
₉

for about a year. She owns a small advertising business. We (*already*) _____

_____ many fun evenings together.
₁₀

▶ **Practice 11. Review: irregular verbs.** (Charts 2-4, 2-5, and 4-4)
Complete the sentences with the correct verb from the list. Use the present perfect tense.

begin	drink	meet	✓put
buy	find	pay	win

1. I _____*have*_____ just _____*put*_____ the dinner in the oven. It will be ready in twenty
   minutes.

2. Stuart is very thirsty from playing tennis in the hot sun. He _____ three
   glasses of water already, and he is asking for more.

3. Hurry, Sal. The program _____ already _____. We can clean up
   the kitchen later.

4. Our basketball team _____ every game so far this season. What a great team!

5. I _____ the president twice. He said, "It's good to meet you. Thank you for
   your support."

6. Two police officers _____ just _____ the missing boy, and they
   are taking him home to his family.

---

punk rocker = someone who likes loud punk music and wears things that are typical of it, such as torn clothes, metal chains, and
colored hair.

7. This bill is a mistake. I _____ already _____ this bill.

8. The new electric car is a big success. Thousands of people _____ one, and many more customers are waiting to buy one.

▶ **Practice 12. Simple past vs. present perfect.** (Chart 4-5)
Write "F" if the activity or situation is finished and "C" if it continues to the present.

1. _C_ My grandfather has worked since he was in high school.
2. _F_ My grandmother worked for 20 years.
3. _F_ I finished my work two hours ago.
4. _F_ I have already finished my work, so I'm leaving the office.
5. ____ My father has been sick since yesterday.
6. ____ Jane was sick last Monday.
7. ____ Tom has already left. He's not here.
8. ____ Tom left five minutes ago.
9. ____ I have known Max Shell since we were children.
10. ____ The baby has had a fever since midnight. I think I'll call the doctor.
11. ____ The baby had a fever all night, but he's better now.
12. ____ I had the flu last year.
13. ____ Sue has had the flu since last Friday.
14. ____ Claude has slept outside under the stars several times this summer.

▶ **Practice 13. Present perfect and simple past with time words.** (Charts 4-1 → 4-5)
Choose (✓) all the phrases that correctly complete the sentences.

1. The Petersons took a trip ____.

____ a. two weeks ago

____ b. since yesterday

____ c. yesterday

____ d. last year

____ e. several months ago

____ f. since last month

____ g. the day before yesterday

____ h. in March

____ i. since winter began

2. The Petersons have been out of town ____.

____ a. the day before yesterday

____ b. one month ago

____ c. since Friday

____ d. last week

____ e. since winter began

____ f. since last week

____ g. in April last year

____ h. several weeks ago

____ i. for several weeks

▶ **Practice 14. Simple past vs. present perfect.** (Chart 4-5)
Complete the sentences with the letter of the correct verbs in the list.

a. paid   g. have paid
b. sent   h. have sent
c. met   i. have met
d. took   j. have taken
e. watched   k. have watched
f. withdrew   l. have withdrawn

1. I __c__ many new people at the conference last week. I __i__ a lot of new people since I started going to conferences ten years ago.

2. I ____ a lot of good movies on TV in my lifetime. I ____ an excellent new movie last night.

3. I ____ my rent this morning. I ____ my rent on time for twenty years.

4. I ____ lots of difficult tests since I started college. I ____ a very difficult test yesterday in my World History class.

5. I ____ more than a thousand dollars from my bank account so far this month. Yesterday I ____ three hundred dollars.

6. I ____ several emails to my friends last night. I ____ thousands of emails to my friends in my lifetime.

▶ **Practice 15. Simple past vs. present perfect.** (Chart 4-5)
Complete the sentences with the correct verb in parentheses. Notice the time expressions.

The Okay Candy Company

(1) The Okay Candy Company is 100 years old this year. The Foxworthy family (*started / has started*) this business in 1910. In the beginning, the company (*was / has been*) small and (*had / has had*) about 20 employees. Now the company (*became / has become*) much larger, and it has more than 200 employees. It (*was / has been*) a very successful company for many years because of good management.

(2) The current president, Oscar M. Foxworthy, (*led / has led*) the company for the last eleven years. The company (*made / has made*) a profit every year since he first (*took / has taken*) over the company. Last year, for example, the company's profits (*went / have gone*) up 4%, and this year profits (*went / have gone*) up 4.2% since January. The year (*didn't end / hasn't ended*) yet, and people are optimistic about the future of the company.

► **Practice 16. Present perfect progressive.** (Chart 4-6)
Complete the sentences with the correct form of the present perfect progressive verb and the appropriate time phrase.

1. I am waiting for the downtown bus. I arrived at the bus stop twenty minutes ago.

   I ____*have been waiting*____ for the bus for _____*twenty minutes*_____ .

2. Sandy is watching TV. She turned on the TV two hours ago.

   She _____ TV for _____ .

3. Ivo is working at the hospital. He began working at 7:00 this morning, and he hasn't stopped. It is now 10 P.M.

   Ivo _____ at the hospital since _____ .

4. Kim is driving. He got in his car six hours ago, and he hasn't stopped.

   Kim _____ for _____ .

5. Ruth is writing a novel. She began it three years ago, and she hasn't finished it yet.

   Ruth _____ the novel for _____ .

6. Jim and Dan are arguing. They began their argument when Jim brought home a stray cat.

   Jim and Dan _____ since _____

   _____ .

7. It began to rain two days ago. It is still raining.

   It _____ for _____ .

8. Jenny is losing weight. She began her diet on her birthday.

   She _____ weight since _____ .

► **Practice 17. Present perfect progressive vs. present perfect.** (Charts 4-6 and 4-7)
Read the passage about Max. Then answer the questions that follow. Circle "T" if the statement is true, and "F" if the statement is false.

Max has written four books. Three of his books did not sell well. The fourth, however, — called *A Tiger's Life* — has been very successful. In fact, right now a production company in Hollywood is making a movie of *A Tiger's Life*. Max is taking a break from writing and is a consultant for the movie. He hasn't written anything new for about a year because he has been working on the movie.

1. Max is writing a book now.   T   F
2. All four of his books have been successful.   T   F
3. *A Tiger's Life* has been a success.   T   F
4. A production company has already made a movie of *A Tiger's Life*.   T   F
5. Max began working on the movie about a year ago.   T   F
6. Max has finished working on the movie.   T   F

► **Practice 18. Present progressive, present perfect progressive and the present perfect.** (Charts 4-6 and 4-7)
Choose the correct verb.

1. Where have you been? The boss ____ for you for over an hour!
   a. is looking   (b.) has been looking

2. I'm exhausted! I _____ for the last eight hours without a break.
   a. am working   b. have been working

3. Shhh! Susan _____ now. Let's not make any noise. We don't want to wake her up.
   a. is sleeping   b. has been sleeping

4. Annie, go upstairs and wake your brother up. He _____ for over ten hours. He has chores to do.
   a. is sleeping   b. has been sleeping

5. Erin has never gone camping. She _____ in a tent.
   a. has never slept   b. has never been sleeping

6. This is a great shirt! I _____ it at least a dozen times, and it still looks like new.
   a. have washed   b. have been washing

7. Are you still washing the dishes? You _____ dishes for thirty minutes. How long can it take to wash dishes?
   a. have washed   b. have been washing

8. We _____ to the Steak House restaurant many times. The food is excellent.
   a. have gone   b. have been going

▶ **Practice 19. Present perfect progressive vs. present perfect.** (Charts 4-6 and 4-7)
Complete the passage with either the present perfect or present perfect progressive form of the verbs from the lists. More than one verb form may be correct.

Global Warming

get   know

The earth _____ warmer for many years, as most people realize.
                        1
And the temperatures will continue to increase. People in the Arctic regions

_____ this for a long time: In those regions, the winters are shorter than they
        2
used to be and the ice in the ocean has become thinner.

become   collect   rise   study

Scientists _____ the climate in the Arctic for many
                        3
years, and they will continue to study it. These scientists _____ a lot
                                                                              4
of information about climate change. For example, air temperatures in the Arctic are getting

warmer. They _____ 5° Celsius since 1910. Another result is that the Arctic
                        5
sea ice is melting. It _____ 40 percent thinner since 1970.
                        6

▶ **Practice 20. Verb tense review.** (Chapters 1–3, and Chart 4-1 → 4-7)
Complete the sentences with the words in parentheses.

Looking for a Job

BEN: I (need) _____*need*_____ to find a job. Where (be) _____ a good place for a
            ₁   ₂
student to work?

ANN: (you, work, ever) _____ at a restaurant?
            ₃

BEN: Yes. I (work) _____ at several restaurants. I (have) _____ a
            ₄   ₅
job as a dishwasher last fall.

ANN: Where?

BEN: At The Bistro, a little café on First Street.

ANN: How long (you, work) _____ there?
            ₆

BEN: For two months.

ANN: I (work) _____ in a lot of restaurants, but I (have, never)
            ₇
_____ a dishwashing job. How (you, like)
            ₈
_____ your job as a dishwasher?
            ₉

BEN: I (like, not) _____ it very much. It (be) _____ hard
            ₁₀   ₁₁
work for low pay.

ANN: Where (you, work) _____ right now?
            ₁₂

BEN: I (have, not) _____ a job right now. I (have, not)
            ₁₃
_____ a job since I (quit) _____ the dishwashing one.
            ₁₄   ₁₅

ANN: (you, look) _____ for a part-time or a full-time job now?
            ₁₆

BEN: A part-time job, maybe twenty hours a week.

ANN: I (go) _____ to Al's Place tomorrow to see about a job. The
            ₁₇
restaurant (look) _____ for help. Why don't you come along
            ₁₈
with me?

BEN: Thanks. I (do) _____ that. I (look, never)
                       19

_____ for a job at Al's Place before. Maybe the pay (be)
                       20

_____ better than at The Bistro.
          21

ANN: I (know, not) _____. We (find) _____ out when
                   22   23

we (go) _____ there tomorrow.
         24

▶ **Practice 21. Past perfect.** (Chart 4-8)
For each item, write "1" before the action that happened first. Write "2" before the action that happened second.

1. Larry called Jane last night, but she had gone out for the evening.

   <u>2</u> Larry called Jane.

   <u>1</u> Jane went out.

2. I opened the door because someone had knocked on it. But no one was there.

   ___ I opened the door.

   ___ Someone knocked on the door.

3. My sister was happy because her boyfriend had called.

   ___ Her boyfriend called.

   ___ My sister was happy.

4. Our dog stood excitedly at the front door. He had seen me as I was putting on my coat to go out for a walk.

   ___ He saw me putting on my coat.

   ___ Our dog stood at the front door.

5. Ken had heard my joke a hundred times before. But he laughed anyway.

   ___ Ken laughed at my joke.

   ___ Ken heard the joke many times.

6. Don opened his car door with a wire hanger. He had lost his keys.

   ___ Don lost his keys.

   ___ Don opened his car door with a wire hanger.

▶ **Practice 22. Past perfect.** (Chart 4-8)
Read the passage and <u>underline</u> the past perfect verbs and the modifying adverbs ***always*** and ***never***. Then complete the sentences that follow the passage. Use the past perfect in your completions.

A New Life for Alan

(1) Alan Green got married for the first time at age 49. His new life is very different because he has had to change many old habits. For example, before his marriage, he <u>had always watched</u> TV during dinner, but his wife likes to talk at dinnertime, so now the TV is off.

(2) Until his marriage, Alan had always read the front page of the newspaper first, but his wife likes to read the front page first too, so now Alan reads the sports page first.

(3) Until he got married, he had never let anyone else choose the radio station in the car. He had always listened to exactly what he wanted to listen to. But his wife likes to choose what's on the radio when she's in the car with him.

(4) When he was a bachelor, Alan had always left his dirty socks on the floor. Now he picks them up and puts them in the laundry basket.

(5) Before he was married, he'd never put the cap back on the toothpaste. He left it off. His wife prefers to have the cap back on. She also squeezes from the bottom of the tube, and Alan doesn't. Alan can't remember to put the cap back on, so now they have separate toothpaste tubes.

(6) Alan had never shared the TV remote control with anyone before he got married. He still likes to have control of the TV remote, but he doesn't say anything when his wife uses it.

Complete these sentences.

1. Until Alan got married, he _____*had always watched*_____ TV during dinner.

2. Before his marriage, he _____ the front page of the newspaper first.

3. Before he got married, he _____ other people choose the station on his car radio.

4. Until he began married life, he _____ his dirty socks on the floor.

5. Before his marriage, he _____ the toothpaste cap back on.

6. Until he had a wife who also liked to use the TV remote control, he _____ the remote with anyone.

▶ **Practice 23. Review of time expressions.** (Chapter 4)
Choose the correct completions.

1. Sacha is sleeping ____.
2. I have called Martin ____ this evening, but he hasn't answered the phone.
3. I'll call Martin one more time ____.
4. Where's Hal? I hope he hasn't gone home ____.
5. My family has lived in this house ____.
6. How many people have lived on earth ____?

a. since the world began
b. for twenty-one years
c. at this moment
d. yet
e. after the 11:00 P.M. news
f. five times

▶ **Practice 24. Verb tense review.** (Chapters 1–4)
Choose the correct verbs.

1. A: (*Did you enjoy* / *Have you enjoyed*) the concert last night?
   B: Oh, yes. I (*have enjoyed* / *enjoyed*) it very much.

2. A: (*Did you see* / *Have you seen*) John yesterday?
   B: Yes, I did. It (*was* / *has been*) good to see him again. I (*haven't seen* / *hadn't seen*) him in a long time.

3. A: Hi, Jim! It's good to see you again. I (*haven't seen* / *didn't see*) you in weeks.
   B: Hi, Sue! It (*was* / *is*) good to see you again, too. I (*haven't seen* / *don't see*) you since the end of last semester. How's everything going?

4. A: (*Did you get* / *Have you gotten*) to class on time yesterday morning?
   B: No. When I (*get* / *got*) there, class (*has already begun* / *had already begun*).

5. A: I called Ana, but I couldn't talk to her.

    B: Why not?

    A: She (*had already gone / has already gone*) to bed, and her sister didn't want to wake her up for a phone call.

6. A: You're a wonderful artist. I love your paintings of the valley.

    B: Thank you. I (*have painted / was painting*) the same valley many times because it has such interesting light at different times of the day.

7. A: How many pictures of the valley (*have you painted / are you painting*) so far?

    B: Oh, more than twenty.

8. A: I see that you (*have been painting / were painting*) when I (*walked / have walked*) in.

    B: Yes. I (*have painted / have been painting*) since early this morning.

▶ **Practice 25. Editing.** (Chapters 1 → 4)
Correct the errors.

                    have been
1. Where were you? I ~~am~~ waiting for you for an hour.

2. Anna have been a soccer fan since a long time.

3. Since I have been a child, I have liked to solve puzzles.

4. Have you ever want to travel around the world?

5. The family is at the hospital since they hear about the accident.

6. My sister is only 30 years old, but her hair has began to turn gray.

7. Jake has been working as a volunteer at the children's hospital since several years.

8. Steve has worn his black suit only once since he has bought it.

9. My cousin is studying for medical school exams since last month.

10. I don't know the results of my medical tests already. I'll find out soon.

11. The phone has already stopped ringing when Michelle entered her apartment.

▶ **Practice 26. Word search puzzle.**

Circle the irregular past participles of these verbs in the puzzle: *become, break, find, go, know, see, take, understand.* Use the clues below the puzzle to help you. The words may be horizontal, vertical, or diagonal. The first letter of each word is highlighted in gray.

U	N	F	P	N	T	A	K	E	N
L	N	W	Q	L	K	L	Y	D	T
F	N	D	O	M	R	Q	D	N	F
D	E	R	E	N	T	C	L	O	H
M	K	H	M	R	K	M	U	T	B
X	O	C	N	M	S	N	Y	E	K
G	R	S	K	T	D	T	N	F	M
J	B	E	R	N	J	O	O	R	W
Y	D	E	P	L	G	M	M	O	L
Q	T	N	E	M	O	C	E	B	D

1. Traffic in this city has _____ very bad recently.

2. I have _____ this bus every morning since I started my new job.

3. How long have you _____ Ali's family?

4. This is a terrible washing machine. It has _____ again.

5. I love that movie. I have _____ it seven times.

6. Is Beth still here? Or has she _____ home already?

7. Hal lost his keys. He hasn't _____ them yet.

8. I am not good at math. I have never _____ those complicated math problems.

Chapter 5
Asking Questions

▶ **Practice 1. Short answers for yes/no questions.** (Chart 5-1)
Read the interview and circle the correct completions.

Job Interview

1. ANA LOPEZ: Hello! I'm looking for the biochemistry department. There's no number on the door. Is this the right place?

   PROFESSOR HIATT: Yes, it _____.
   a. does   b. has   c. is

2. PROF: And you must be the student who called for an interview! Are you Ana Lopez?

   ANA: Yes, I _____.
   a. do   b. am   c. have

3. PROF: I'm Professor Hiatt. It's nice to meet you. Welcome to the biochemistry department.

   ANA: Thank you. I'm very glad to meet you.

   PROF: Well, first of all, we want an assistant who really likes to work on research projects in the lab. Do you like that kind of work?

   ANA: Yes, I _____. I like it very much.
   a. do   b. am   c. have

4. PROF: Good. Have you had a lot of experience in a biochemistry lab?

   ANA: Yes, I _____. I worked as the student assistant in high school. And I also worked at a small chemical company for two summers.
   a. do   b. am   c. have

   PROF: Did you work on any research projects at that company?

   ANA: Yes, I _____. I assisted two chemists in medical research.
   a. did   b. have   c. do

5. PROF: Now, are you taking a lot of classes this semester?

   ANA: Yes, I _____. I'm taking biology, statistics, and two chemistry courses.
   a. do   b. am   c. will

6. PROF: Those are difficult classes. Will you have time to study and work here in the lab too?

   ANA: Yes, I _____.
   a. do   b. will   c. have

▶ **Practice 2. Yes/no questions.** (Chart 5-1)
Make questions using the information in B's response.

	helping verb	subject	main verb	rest of sentence
1. **SIMPLE** A:	Do	you	like	coffee?
PRESENT B:	Yes, I like coffee.			

	helping verb	subject	main verb	rest of sentence
2. **SIMPLE** A:	_____	_____	_____	_____
PRESENT B:	Yes, Tom likes coffee.			

	helping verb	subject	main verb	rest of sentence
3. **PRESENT** A:	_____	_____	_____	_____
PROGRESSIVE B:	Yes, Pietro is watching TV.			

	helping verb	subject	main verb	rest of sentence
4. **PRESENT** A:	_____	_____	_____	_____
PROGRESSIVE B:	Yes, I'm having lunch with Raja.			

	helping verb	subject	main verb	rest of sentence
5. **SIMPLE** A:	_____	_____	_____	_____
PAST B:	Yes, Rafael walked to school.			

	helping verb	subject	main verb	rest of sentence
6. **PAST** A:	_____	_____	_____	_____
PROGRESSIVE B:	Yes, Clarita was taking a nap.			

	helping verb	subject	main verb	rest of sentence
7. **SIMPLE** A:	_____	_____	_____	_____
FUTURE B:	Yes, Ted will come to the meeting.			

	form of *be*	subject	rest of sentence
8. **MAIN VERB:** *BE* A:	_____	_____	_____
SIMPLE B:	Yes, Ingrid is a good artist.		
PRESENT			

	form of *be*	subject	rest of sentence
9. **MAIN VERB:** *BE* A:	_____	_____	_____
SIMPLE PAST B:	Yes, I was at the wedding.		

► **Practice 3. Yes/no questions and short answers.** (Chart 5-1)
Choose the correct completions.

1. A: (*Is* / *Does*) this your new laptop?
   B: Yes, it (*is* / *does*).

2. A: It's so small. (*Is* / *Does*) it difficult to see text on that tiny screen?
   B: No, it (*isn't* / *doesn't*).

3. A: (*Is* / *Does*) it run on a battery?
   B: Yes, it (*has* / *does*).

4. A: (*Do* / *Are*) you carry it with you all day?
   B: Yes, I (*am* / *do*).

5. A: (*Have* / *Do*) you had it for a long time?
   B: No, I (*haven't* / *don't*).

6. A: (*Was* / *Did*) it cost a lot?
   B: No, it (*wasn't* / *didn't*).

7. A: (*Are* / *Do*) you going to take it on your trip to Africa?
   B: Yes, I (*am* / *do*).

8. A: (*Are* / *Will*) you send emails from Africa ?
   B: Yes, I (*am* / *will*).

► **Practice 4. Yes/no questions and short answers.** (Chart 5-1)
Complete the conversations. Use the correct forms of **be**, **do**, **have**, or **will**.

1. A: I need a map. _____*Do*_____ you have one?
   B: No, I _____*don't*_____ .

2. A: _____*Are*_____ the Andes Mountains in North America?
   B: No, they _____*aren't*_____ .

3. A: _____ Africa the largest continent?
   B: No, it _____ . Asia is.

4. A: _____ rivers flow toward the oceans?
   B: Yes, they _____ .

5. A: _____ penguins live in the Arctic?
   B: No, they _____ . They live in Antarctica.

6. A: _____ a penguin swim under water?
   B: Yes, it _____ .

7. A: _____ the Nile the longest river in the world?
   B: Yes, it _____ .

8. A: _____ it snow in Hawaii?
   B: No, it _____ . It's too warm there for snow.

9. A: _____ 2029 be a leap year?

    B: No, it _____. A leap year is a year that you can divide by 4, like 2012, 2016, and 2020.

▶ **Practice 5. Yes/no questions.** (Chart 5-1)
The chart describes the exam schedule of four students. Complete the conversations using the information in the chart.

	Last week	**This week**	**Next week**
Jane		math	computer science
George	Spanish		business
Anna		biology	chemistry
John	history		

1. A: _____*Does Jane*_____ have an exam this week?

    B: Yes, _____*she does.*_____ (Jane has an exam this week.)

2. A: _____ have an exam this week?

    B: No, _____. (George doesn't have an exam this week.)

3. A: _____ have exams this week?

    B: Yes, _____. (Jane and Anna have exams this week.)

4. A: _____ have an exam last week?

    B: No, _____. (Jane didn't have an exam last week.)

5. A: _____ have an exam last week?

    B: Yes, _____. (George had an exam last week.)

6. A: _____ have exams last week?

    B: No, _____. (Jane and Anna didn't have exams last week.)

7. A: _____ have exams last week?

    B: Yes, _____. (George and John had exams last week.)

8. A: _____ have an exam next week?

    B: Yes, _____. (Jane will have an exam next week.)

9. A: _____ have an exam next week?

    B: Yes, _____. (George and Anna will have exams next week.)

10. A: _____ have an exam next week?

    B: No, _____. (John will not have an exam next week.)

► **Practice 6. Forming information questions.** (Chart 5-2)
Choose the correct completion.

1. Phil works **someplace**.

    Where (*works Phil* / *does Phil work*) ?

2. He works **sometimes**.

    When (*does Phil work* / *works Phil*) ?

3. Marta is making **something**.

    What (*Marta is making* / *is Marta making*) ?

4. She said **something**.

    What (*did she say* / *she said*) ?

5. Jean and Don visited **someone**.

    Who (*Jean and Don did visit* / *did Jean and Don visit*) ?

6. They visited her **for a reason**.

    Why (*did they visit her* / *they visited her*) ?

► **Practice 7. Yes/no and information questions.** (Charts 5-1 and 5-2)
Complete the sentences with words from the list.

Does	Is	When	Where

1. _____ Marvin work in a restaurant?
2. _____ does Marvin work? Downtown?
3. _____ Marvin working today?
4. _____ does Marvin have a day off? On Saturday?

Are	Will	When	Where

5. _____ Mike and Kate get married next year?
6. _____ will Mike and Kate get married? Soon?
7. _____ they going to have a honeymoon?
8. _____ are they going to go on their honeymoon? Hawaii?

Did	Is	When	Where

9. _____ Iris in class now?
10. _____ is Iris?
11. _____ she come to class yesterday?
12. _____ will Iris come back to class?

► **Practice 8. Yes/no and information questions.** (Charts 5-1 and 5-2)
Make questions using the information in B's response. Write Ø if no word is needed.

	(question word)	helping verb	subject	main verb	rest of sentence
1. A:	Ø	Did	you	hear	the news yesterday?

B: Yes, I did. (I heard the news yesterday.)

	(question word)	helping verb	subject	main verb	rest of sentence
2. A:	When	did	you	hear	the news?

B: Yesterday. (I heard the news yesterday.)

	(question word)	helping verb	subject	main verb	rest of sentence
3. A:	Ø				

B: Yes, he is. (Eric is traveling in South America.)

	(question word)	helping verb	subject	main verb	rest of sentence
4. A:					Ø

B: In South America. (Eric is traveling in South America.)

	(question word)	helping verb	subject	main verb	rest of sentence
5. A:					

B: Yes, it will. (The class will end in December.)

	(question word)	helping verb	subject	main verb	rest of sentence
6. A:					

B: In December. (The class will end in December.)

	(question word)	helping verb	subject	main verb	rest of sentence
7. A:					

B: Yes, she did. (The teacher helped a student.)

	(question word)	helping verb	subject	main verb	rest of sentence
8. A:					

B: Mei Lei. (The teacher helped Mei Lei.)

	(question word)	helping verb	subject	main verb	rest of sentence
9. A:					

B: Yes, he will. (The chef will cook his special chicken dinner tonight.)

	(question word)	helping verb	subject	main verb	rest of sentence
10. A:					

B: His special chicken dinner. (The chef will cook his special chicken dinner tonight.)

► **Practice 9. Yes/no and information questions.** (Charts 5-1 and 5-2)
Read the passage. Then write questions using the given words, and circle the correct answers.
Capitalize the first word of the question.

Apples

Apple trees first grew in central Asia thousands of years ago. Today apples grow in cooler climates all over the world. Each spring, apple trees produce pink flowers. In the summer and fall, the trees produce apples. Inside each apple there are tiny brown seeds. If you plant these seeds, some of them will become new apple trees.

1. *did, originate, apple trees, where*

    _____Where did apple trees originate_____?

    a. Yes, they did.   b. In central Asia.

2. *do, where, grow, apple trees*

    _____?

    a. Yes, they do.   b. In cooler climates everywhere.

3. *they, do, grow*

    _____ in hot climates?

    a. No, they don't.   b. In central Asia.

4. *do, apples, the trees, produce*

    _____ in the summer and fall?

    a. Yes, they do.   b. Apples.

5. *produce, do, they, when*

    _____ pink flowers?

    a. Yes, they do.   b. In the spring.

6. *what, find, you, do*

    _____ inside each apple?

    a. Yes, you do.   b. Seeds.

7. *some of the seeds, become, will*

    _____ new apple trees?

    a. Yes, they will.   b. New apple seeds.

▶ **Practice 10. *Where, When, What time, Why, How come, What . . . for.***
(Chart 5-3)
For each question, write the correct completion from Column B.

Column A

Column B

1. _____ do oranges come from?
   Florida.

2. _____ is the sky blue?
   Because the sun reflects the light in a certain way.

3. _____ did the 21st century begin?
   In the year 2000.

4. _____ is the flight going to arrive?
   At 5:30.

5. _____ you left early?
   I went to the dentist.

6. _____ did you go to the dentist for?
   I had a bad toothache.

a. What

b. What time

c. When

d. Where

e. Why

f. How come

▶ **Practice 11. *Why, How come, and What for.*** (Chart 5-3)
Rewrite the sentences beginning with the given words.

1. What are you going downtown for?
   a. How come _____?
   b. Why _____?

2. Why did Paul leave early?
   a. What _____?
   b. How come _____?

3. How come your clothes are on the floor?
   a. Why _____?
   b What _____?

4. What does Mira need more money for?
   a. How come _____?
   b. Why _____?

▶ **Practice 12. *Where, Why, When, and What time.*** (Chart 5-3)
Make information questions. Use ***where*, *why*, *when*, or *what time***. Use the information in parentheses in your question.

1. A: _____ to see the principal?
   B: Because I need his signature on this application. (I'm waiting to see the principal because I need his signature on this application.)

2. A: _____ her new job?
   B: Next Monday morning. (Rachel starts her new job next Monday morning.)

3. A: _____ the business meeting?
   B: Because I fell asleep after dinner and didn't wake up until 9:00. (I missed the meeting because I fell asleep after dinner and didn't wake up until 9:00.)

4. A: _____ for home?
   B: Next Saturday. (I'm leaving for home next Saturday.)

5. A: _____ to finish this project?
   B: Next month. (I expect to finish this project next month.)

6. A: _____ today?
   B: At the cafeteria. (I ate lunch at the cafeteria today.)

7. A: _____ lunch?
   B: At 12:15. (I ate lunch at 12:15.)

8. A: _____ at the cafeteria?
   B: Because the food is good. (I eat lunch at the cafeteria because the food is good.)

9. A: _____?
   B: From Osaka to Tokyo. (The bullet train goes from Osaka to Tokyo.)

10. A: _____
    from New York to Los Angeles ?
    B: One day in the future, I think! (They will build a bullet train from New York to Los Angeles one day in the future.)

11. A: _____ English?
    B: In Germany. (I studied English in Germany.)

12. A: _____ English in Germany?
    B: Because I had a scholarship to study in Germany. (I studied English in Germany because I had a scholarship to study in Germany.)

▶ **Practice 13. *Who, Who(m),* and *What.*** (Chart 5-4)
Write "S" over the boldface word if it is the subject of the verb. Write "O" over the word if it is the object of the verb. Then make questions with ***who, who*(*m*), and *what*.**

1. **Someone** is talking.
            S
   _____Who is talking_____?

2. We hear **someone**.
            O
   _____Who(m) do we hear_____?

3. You know **someone** in my class.
   _____ in my class?

4. **Someone** was on TV last night.
   _____ last night?

5. **Something** is happening in that building.
   _____ in that building?

6. Jason knows **something**.

   _____,_____?

7. Gilda called **someone**.

   _____?

8. **Someone** answered the phone.

   _____?

9. You said **something**.

   _____?

10. **Something** is important.

    _____?

▶ **Practice 14. Who, Who(m), and What.** (Chart 5-4)
Complete the questions with **who**, **who(m)**, or **what**.
Part I. Looking for the subject.

At an Office Meeting

1. _____ happened at the meeting?
2. _____ was there?
3. _____ spoke about the reorganization of the company?
4. _____ is going on in the finance department?
5. _____ is going to be the next chief financial officer?
6. _____ is the problem with the air-conditioning system?

Part II. Looking for the object.

Planning a Dinner Party

1. _____ are you inviting to dinner?
2. _____ has already responded?
3. _____ are you going to serve, meat or fish?
4. _____ do you need to buy for the dinner?
5. _____ are you going to make for dessert?
6. _____ do you need me to do?

▶ **Practice 15. Who, Who(m), and What.** (Chart 5-4)
Make questions with **who**, **who(m)**, and **what**.

	QUESTION	ANSWER
1.	_Who knows Julio?_	**Someone** knows Julio.
2.	_Who(m) does Julio know?_	Julio knows **someone**.
3.	_____	**Someone** will help us.
4.	_____	I will ask **someone**.
5.	_____	Eric is talking to **someone** on the phone.
6.	_____	**Someone** is knocking on the door.

7. _____ **Something** surprised them.

8. _____ Jack said **something**.

9. _____ Sue talked about **something**.

10. _____ Rosa talked about **someone**.

▶ **Practice 16. Who, Who(m), and What.** (Chart 5-4)
Make questions using the information in parentheses.

1. A: _____Who taught_____ you to play chess?
   B: My mother. (My mother taught me to play chess.)

2. A: _____?
   B: A bank robbery. (Robert saw a bank robbery.)

3. A: _____ a good look at the bank robber?
   B: Robert did. (Robert got a good look at the bank robber.)

4. A: _____?
   B: A toy for my brother's children. (I'm making a toy for my brother's children.)

5. A: _____ to?
   B: Joe. (That cell phone belongs to Joe.)

6. A: _____ on the front window of your car?
   B: A parking ticket. (A parking ticket is on the front window of my car.)

▶ **Practice 17. Asking for the meaning of a word.** (Chart 5-4)
Ask for the meaning of the words in *italics*. Complete the conversations in your own words.

1. A: Jenny is going to study *abroad* next year.
   B: What _____does "abroad" mean_____?
   It means _____in a foreign country_____.

2. A: The kitten is hiding *underneath* the blanket.
   B: _____?
   A: It means _____.

3. A: The weather this winter has been *mild*.
   B: _____?
   A: It means _____.

4. A: Todd thinks I'm *cool*.
   B: _____?
   A: It means _____.

5. A: My boss says that I'm *industrious*.
   B: _____?
   A: It means _____.

► **Practice 18. *What* + a form of *do*.** (Chart 5-5)
Make questions using ***what*** and a form of ***do***. Use the information in parentheses. Use the same verb tense that is <u>underlined</u> in parentheses.

1. A: _____*What is Alex doing*_____ now?
   B: Watching a movie on TV. (Alex <u>is watching</u> a movie on TV.)

2. A: _____ last weekend?
   B: Nothing. We just stayed home. (We did nothing last weekend. We just <u>stayed</u> home.)

3. A: _____?
   B: They explore space. (Astronauts <u>explore</u> space.)

4. A: _____ next Saturday morning?
   B: Play tennis at Waterfall Park.
   (I'<u>m going to play</u> tennis at Waterfall Park next Saturday morning.)

5. A: _____ when she heard the good news?
   B: She cried with happiness. (Sara <u>cried</u> with happiness when she heard the good news.)

6. A: _____ after she graduates?
   B: I think she plans to look for a job in hotel management. (Emily <u>is going to look</u> for a job in hotel management after she graduates.)

7. A: _____ after school today?
   B: Let's go to the mall, okay? (I <u>want</u> to go to the mall after school today.)

8. A: _____ for a living?
   B: He's an airplane mechanic. (Nick <u>repairs</u> airplanes for a living.)

► **Practice 19. Using *which* and *what*.** (Chart 5-6)
Choose the correct word in each sentence.

1. A: Ali broke his hand playing basketball.
   B: That's terrible. (*Which* /*What*) hand did he break, the right or left?

2. A: I heard the president's speech last night. Did you?
   B: No, I didn't. (*Which* /*What*) did he say about the economy?

3. A: This book is excellent. It's the best book I have ever read.
   B: Really? (*Which* /*What*) is it about?

4. A: Look at those two pandas! They are so cute.
   B: They are. (*Which* /*What*) one is the mother and (*which* / *what*) one is the daughter?

5. A: We have an invitation to the art show on Friday night.
   B: I'd like to go. But I've never been to an art show before. (*Which* /*What*) do people wear to art shows?

6. A: Alec lives on this street, right?
   B: This is the street, but (*which* / *what*) house is it? Do you have the exact address?

7. A: I don't have the address.
   B: Let's call him. (*Which* /*What*) is his phone number?

8. A: Hey, Bernie! I'm surprised to see you here.

   B: Hey, Marty! (*Which / What*) are you doing these days?

   A: Me? Not much. But my son just got an offer from the Broilers to play professional soccer on their team.

   B: That's great! Uh . . . (*which / what*) son is that? Is it Jeff?

   A: No. Jeff's in medical school. I'm talking about Alan, my youngest.

▶ **Practice 20. Using *which* and *what kind of*.** (Chart 5-6)
Make questions with ***what kind of*** and one of the nouns in the list for each question.

books	clothes	Italian food	✓music
car	government	job	person

1. A: _____ *What kind of music* _____ do you like?

   B: Rock 'n roll.

2. A: _____ do you usually wear?

   B: Jeans and a T-shirt.

3. A: _____ do you like best?

   B: Pizza with double cheese, onions, peppers, and garlic.

4. A: _____ do you like to read?

   B: Romance novels.

5. A: _____ are you going to buy?

   B: A hybrid. One that uses a battery and gas.

6. A: _____ does your country have?

   B: It's a democratic republic.

7. A: _____ would you like to have?

   B: I'd like to have one that pays well, is interesting, and allows me to travel a lot.

8. A: _____ would you like to marry?

   B: Someone who is kind-hearted, loving, funny, serious, and steady.

▶ **Practice 21. *Who* vs. *Whose*.** (Chart 5-7)
Complete the questions with ***who*** or ***whose***.

1. A: _____ *Who* _____ is driving to the game tonight?

   B: Heidi is.

2. A: _____ *Whose* _____ car are we taking to the game?

   B: Heidi's.

3. A: This notebook is mine. _____ is that? Is it yours?

   B: No, it's Sara's.

4. A: There's Ms. Adams. _____ is standing next to her?

   B: Mr. Wilson.

5. A: _____ was the first woman doctor in the United States?

   B: Elizabeth Blackwell. She became a doctor in 1849.

6. A: _____ forgot to put the ice cream back in the freezer?

   B: I don't know. It wasn't me!

7. A: _____ suitcase did you borrow for your trip?

   B: Andy's.

▶ **Practice 22. *Who* vs. *Whose*.** (Chart 5-7)
Make questions with ***who*** or ***whose***.

1. A: _____*Whose house is that?*_____

   B: Pat's. (That's Pat's house.)

2. A: _____*Who's living in that house?*_____

   B: Pat. (Pat is living in that house.)

3. A: _____

   B: Pedro's. (I borrowed Pedro's umbrella.)

4. A: _____

   B: Linda's. (I used Linda's book.)

5. A: _____

   B: Nick's. (Nick's book is on the table.)

6. A: _____

   B: Nick. (Nick is on the phone.)

7. A: _____

   B: Sue Smith. (That's Sue Smith.) She's a student in my class.

8. A: _____

   B: Sue's. (That's Sue's.) This one is mine.

▶ **Practice 23. Using *How*.** (Chart 5-8)
Complete the sentences with appropriate words from the list.

busy	fresh	safe	soon
expensive	✓hot	serious	well

1. A: How _____*hot*_____ does it get in Chicago in the summer?

   B: Very _____*hot*_____. It can get over 100°.*

2. A: How _____ will dinner be ready? I'm really hungry.

   B: In just a few more minutes.

3. A: Look at that beautiful painting! Let's get it.

   B: How _____ is it?

   A: Oh, my gosh! Never mind. We can't afford it.

4. A: How _____ are you today, Ted? Do you have time to read over this report?

   B: Well, I am really _____, but I'll make time to read it.

---

*100°F = 37.8°C

5. A: How _____ is Toshi about becoming an astronomer?

   B: He's very _____ about it. He already knows more about the stars and
   planets than his high school teachers.

6. A: How _____ is a car with an airbag?

   B: Statistics say that cars with airbags are very safe.

7. A: Tomatoes for sale! Do you want to buy some tomatoes?

   B: Hmmm. They look pretty good. How _____ are they?

   A: They are really _____. I picked them myself from the field just this
   morning.

8. A: Do you know Jack Young?

   B: Yes.

   A: Oh? How _____ do you know him?

   B: Very _____. He's one of my closest friends. Why?

   A: He's applied for a job at my store.

▶ **Practice 24. Using *How often.*** (Chart 5-9)
Complete the questions using *how often* or *how many times*.

1. A: (*How often / How many times*) are the summer Olympic Games held?

   B: The summer games are held every four years.

2. A: (*How often / How many times*) have the Olympic Games been held in Australia? One or two?

   B: Two, I think. In 1956 and in 2000.

3. A: (*How often / How many times*) did Michael Phelps compete in the Olympics?

   B: I'm not sure. Maybe three or four.

4. A: (*How often / How many times*) do you take vitamin C?

   B: I take it every day. I think it prevents colds.

5. A: (*How often / How many times*) do you get a cold?

   B: Rarely. I rarely get a cold.

6. A: (*How often / How many times*) a year do you visit your doctor?

   B: Sometimes none! I never see my doctor unless I'm sick.

▶ **Practice 25. Using *How far, It + take,* and *How long.*** (Charts 5-10 and 5-11).
Read each paragraph and write questions. Include the word in parentheses in your question. Use
the correct tenses, according to the paragraph.

1. The Nile River is the longest river in the world. It is about 6,677 kilometers, or 4,150 miles,
   long. It flows from Burundi in eastern Africa to the Mediterranean Sea in northeast Egypt.
   A slow ship takes several days to make the trip.

   A: (*far*) _____ from the beginning, or source, of the
   Nile River to the end of the Nile River?

   B: It's a long way.

A: (*miles*) _____ from the source of the

Nile River to the end of the Nile River?

B: About 4,150.

A: (*long*) _____ a slow ship to make the trip?

B: Several days.

2. Mount Everest is 8,850 meters, or 29,035 feet high — the highest mountain in the world. It is in the central Himalaya Mountains, on the border of Tibet and Nepal. Edmund Hillary and his group climbed to the top of the mountain in 1953. It took them seven weeks to get to the top but only three days to come down.

A: (*high*) _____?

B: It's very high. It's more than 29,000 feet high.

A: (*meters*) _____?

B: It's 8,850.

A: (*long*) _____ Edmund Hillary and his

group to climb Mount Everest?

B: Seven weeks.

A: (*days*) _____ them to come down

from the top of the mountain?

B: Three.

3. The Trans-Siberian Railway is the longest railway in the world. It goes from Moscow to Vladivostok on the Sea of Japan, a distance of 9,311 kilometers, or 5,786 miles. The trip takes seven days.

A: (*long*) _____ the Trans-Siberian Railway?

B: Very long. Over 9,100 kilometers.

A: (*miles*) _____ the Trans-Siberian Railway?

B: It's 5,786.

A: (*days*) _____ to go from Moscow

to Vladivostok on the Trans-Siberian Railway?

B: Seven.

▶ **Practice 26. Using *How often, How far*, and *How long*.** (Charts 5-9 → 5-11)
Complete the questions with *far*, *long*, or *often*.

1. A: How ___*far*___ is it to the nearest police station?
   B: Four blocks.

2. A: How _____ does it take you to get to work?
   B: Forty-five minutes.

3. A: How _____ do you see your family?
   B: Once a week.

4. A: How _____ is it to your office from home?
   B: About twenty miles.

5. A: How _____ is it from here to the airport?
   B: Ten kilometers.

6. A: How _____ docs it take to get to the airport?

   B: Fifteen minutes.

7. A: How _____ above sea level is Denver, Colorado?

   B: One mile. That's why it's called the Mile High City.

8. A: How _____ does it take to fly from Chicago to Denver?

   B: About three hours.

9. A: How _____ does the bus come?

   B: Every two hours.

10. A: How _____ is it from here to the bus stop?

    B: About two blocks.

11. A: How _____ does the ride downtown take?

    B: About twenty minutes.

12. A: How _____ do you take the bus?

    B: Every day.

▶ **Practice 27. More questions with *How*.** (Chart 5-13)
Make simple present tense questions with ***how*** and ***you*** as the subject. Use the verbs in the list only once.

feel	like	pronounce	say	spell

1. A: _____?

   B: I spell my name R-I-C-H-A-R-D.

2. A: _____ your eggs?

   B: I like them scrambled, not too hard.

3. A: _____ *I love you* in French?

   B: *Je t'aime.* That's how you say it.

4. A: _____ *Mississippi*?

   B: This is how you pronounce it: say *missus* – like *Mrs.*, and then say *sip* like *sip a drink with a straw*, and then *E* like the letter *E*.

5. A: _____ about losing your job?

   B: Pretty bad, as you would expect.

▶ **Practice 28. Using *How about* and *What about*.** (Chart 5-13)
Write the letter of the appropriate response for each conversation.

1. A: We aren't taking a vacation this summer. What about you?

   B: _____. Jim can't leave his job right now.

      a. We're staying home too.

      b. No, we didn't.

      c. Oh? Where are you going this year?

2. A: I really don't like our history professor. How about you?

   B: ____.

   - a. I don't feel well today.
   - b. What's the matter with her? I like her a lot.
   - c. Yes, I will.

3. A: I'm voting for the new, young candidate. How about you?

   B: Not me. ____.

   - a. Where are you going?
   - b. I think I will.
   - c. I like the older guy, the one with experience.

4. A: I like sailing and being on the water. I like it a lot. How about you?

   B: ____.

   - a. I love it.
   - b. Yes, I have.
   - c. Yes, I did.

5. A: You don't eat meat, sir? What about fish? We have an excellent salmon tonight.

   B: ____.

   - a. No, thank you. I don't take sugar with my coffee.
   - b. Okay, I'll have that.
   - c. Yes, I am.

6. A: I thought the concert was the best concert I had ever been to. How about you?

   B: ____.

   - a. The book was excellent.
   - b. I like music.
   - c. Me too.

▶ **Practice 29. Review of questions.** (Charts 5-1 → 5-14)
Make questions using the given words.

1. *be, dry, the clothes, will*

   A: When _____*will the clothes be dry*_____?

   B: In about an hour.

2. *did, do, you*

   A: What _____ on Saturday afternoon?

   B: I went to a baseball game.

3. *book, download, did, you*

   A: Which _____?

   B: A novel by Jorge Amado.

4. *did, it, long, take*

   A: How _____ to clean your apartment

   before your parents visited?

   B: Four hours.

5. *bread, do, like, you*

A: What kind of _____?

B: I don't like bread. I never eat it.

6. *are, calling, me, you*

A: Why _____ so late at night ?

B: Sorry! I hit the wrong number on my phone and dialed you by mistake.

7. *are, meeting, you*

A: Who _____ at the restaurant?

B: Maria and her sister.

8. *is, you, taking*

A. Who _____ to the airport?

B: Eric.

9. *are, leaving, you*

A: How come _____ so early?

B: I'm really very tired.

▶ **Practice 30. Review of questions.** (Charts 5-1 → 5-14)
Complete the conversations by writing questions for the given answers. Use the information in parentheses to form the questions.

A Tennis Game

1. A: _____*What is Jack doing*_____ now?
   B: He's playing tennis. (Jack is playing tennis.)

2. A: _____ with?
   B: Anna. (He is playing tennis with Anna.)

3. A: _____?
   B: Serving the ball. (Anna is serving the ball.)

4. A: _____ in the air?
   B: A tennis ball. (She is throwing a tennis ball in the air.)

5. A: _____?
   B: Rackets. (Anna and Jack are holding rackets.)

6. A: _____ between them?
   B: A net. (A net is between them.)

7. A: _____?
   B: On a tennis court. (They are on a tennis court.)

8. A: _____?
   B: For an hour and a half. (They have been playing for an hour and a half.)

9. A: _____ right now?
   B: Jack. (Jack is winning right now.)

10. A: _____ the last game?
    B: Anna. (Anna won the last game.)

▶ **Practice 31. Tag questions.** (Chart 5-15)
Complete the tag questions with the correct verbs.

1. Simple present

   a. You work at the university, _____*don't*_____ you?

   b. Claire teaches at Midwood High School, _____ she?

   c. Bob and Mike sell real estate, _____ they?

   d. Kevin has a van, _____ he?

   e. You're in Professor Rossiter's class, _____ you?

   f. Your mother likes green tea, _____ she?

   g. Jill and Andrew don't have any children yet, _____ they?

   h. Bryan isn't a lawyer, _____ he?

   i. I'm not wrong, _____ I?

2. Simple past

   a. Jennifer went to Mexico, _____ she?

   b. You spoke to Paul about this, _____ you?

   c. That was a good idea, _____ it?

   d. The police officer didn't give you a ticket, _____ he?

   e. John and Mary had a fight, _____ they?

3. Present progressive, *be going to,* and past progressive

   a. You're coming tomorrow, _____ you?

   b. Jim isn't working at the bank, _____ he?

   c. It's probably going to snow tomorrow, _____ it?

   d. Susie was sleeping in class, _____ she?

   e. The printer was working, _____ it?

   f. They weren't leaving, _____ they?

4. Present perfect

   a. The weather has been nice this spring, _____ it?

   b. We've had a lot of work this semester, _____ we?

   c. You haven't told the truth, _____ you?

   d. Shirley has gone home already, _____ she?

   e. Natalie hasn't left yet, _____ she?

   f. I have never met you before, _____ I?

▶ **Practice 32. Tag questions.** (Chart 5-15)
Add tag questions. Write the <u>expected</u> responses.

1. A: You've already seen that movie, _____*haven't you*_____?
   B: _____*Yes, I have*_____.

2. A: John hasn't called, _____?
   B: _____.

3. A: You talked to Mike last night, _____?
   B: _____.

4. A: You usually bring your lunch to school, _____?
   B: _____.

5. A: Rita and Philip have been married for five years, _____?
   B: _____.

6. A: Kathy has already finished her work, _____?
   B: _____.

7. A: This isn't a hard exercise, _____?
   B: _____.

8. A: Tony Wah lives in Los Angeles, _____?
   B: _____.

9. A: Tomorrow isn't a holiday, _____?
   B: _____.

10. A: This isn't your book, _____?
    B: _____.

11. A: Jack and Elizabeth were in class yesterday, _____?
    B: _____.

12. A: Maria won't be here for dinner tonight, _____?
    B: _____.

▶ **Practice 33. Editing.** (Chapter 5)
Correct the errors.

      Who
1. ~~Whom~~ saw the car accident?

2. How about ask Julie and Tim to come for dinner Friday night?

3. What time class begins today?

4. Where people go to get a driver's license in this city?

5. How long it takes to get to the beach from here?

6. She is working late tonight, doesn't she?

7. Who's glasses are those?

8. How much tall your father?

9. Who you talked to about registration for next term?

10. How come are you here so early today?

► **Practice 34. Review: questions.** (Chapter 5)
Make questions using the information in parentheses.

1. A: _____*When are you going to buy*_____ a new bicycle?
   B: Next week. (I'm going to buy a new bicycle next week.)

2. A: _____*How are you going to pay*_____ for it?
   B: With my credit card. (I'm going to pay for it with my credit card.)

3. A: _____ your old bike?
   B: Ten years. (I have had my old bike for ten years.)

4. A: _____ your bike?
   B: Four or five times a week. (I ride my bike four or five times a week.)

5. A: _____ to work?
   B: I usually ride my bike. (I usually get to work by riding my bike.)

6. A: _____ your bike to work today?
   B: No. Today I got a ride. (I didn't ride my bike to work today.)

7. A: Oh. _____ you a ride?
   B: Paul did. (Paul gave me a ride.)

8. A: _____ your bike over the weekend?
   B: Yes, I did. (I rode my bike over the weekend.)

9. A: _____ over the weekend?
   B: Twenty-five miles. (I rode my bike twenty-five miles over the weekend.)

10. A: _____ a comfortable seat?
    B: Yes, it does. (My bike has a comfortable seat.)

11. A: _____?
    B: A ten-speed bike. (I have a ten-speed bike.)

12. A: _____ his new bike?
    B: Two weeks ago. (Jason got his new bike two weeks ago.)

13. A: _____ Jason's new bike?
    B: Billy. (Billy broke Jason's new bike.)

14. A: _____?
    B: He ran it into a brick wall. (He broke it by running it into a brick wall.)

15. A: _____?

    B: No, he didn't. (Billy didn't get hurt.)

16. A: _____?

    B: No, it didn't. Only one wheel fell off. (The bike didn't have a lot of damage.)

17. A: _____?

    B: The front wheel. (The front wheel fell off, not the back wheel.)

18. A: _____?

    B: No, he hasn't. (Jason hasn't fixed the bike yet.)

▶ **Practice 35. Crossword puzzle.** (Chapter 5)
Complete the crossword puzzle. Use the clues to find the correct words.

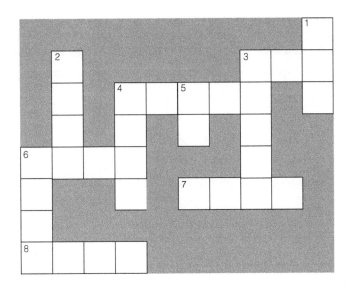

Across

3. I need someone to translate this letter from Chinese. _____ speaks Chinese?

4. _____ hand do you write with, your right or your left?

6. _____ you at home last night? I called, but no one answered.

7. _____ Florida have any mountains?

8. I need to buy some flour. What _____ do the stores open?

Down

1. _____ far is the main road from here?

2. How long does it _____ to go downtown on the bus?

3. _____ are you going now? To your yoga lesson?

4. _____ are you going to return? This afternoon or tonight?

5. _____ Rome the capital of Italy?

6. _____ happened over there? I see several police cars.

Chapter 6
Nouns and Pronouns

▶ **Practice 1. Forms of nouns.** (Chart 6-1)
Read the paragraph. Circle each singular noun. Underline each plural noun.

Sharks

A (shark) is a fish. Sharks live in oceans all over the world. Some types are very large. The largest shark is the size of a bus. It has 3,000 teeth, in five rows in its mouth. When one tooth falls out, a new tooth grows in quickly. Many sharks are dangerous, and people try to avoid them.

▶ **Practice 2. Forms of nouns.** (Chart 6-1)
Write the plural form of the noun under each heading.

apple	child	lamp	river
bed	city	man	shelf
carrot	country	mouse	table
cat	fox	ocean	tomato
cherry	lake	peach	tiger

Living things that breathe	Furniture	Places on a map	Fruits and vegetables

▶ **Practice 3. Forms of nouns.** (Chart 6-1)
Write the correct singular or plural form of the given words.

1. one house   two _____*houses*_____

2. a _____*door*_____   two doors

3. one box   a lot of _____

4. one _____   three shelves

5. a copy   two _____

6. a family   several _____

7. a _____   two women

8. one child   three _____

9. one fish   several _____

10. a _____   a lot of flies

11. a dish   two _____

12. a glass   many _____

13. one _____   two dollars

14. one euro   ten _____

15. a _____   several roofs

16. one life   many _____

17. a radio   a few _____

▶ **Practice 4. Forms of nouns.** (Chart 6-1)
Underline each noun. Write the correct plural if necessary. Do not change any other words.

1. Airplane_∧^s have wing_∧^s.

2. Some baby are born with a few tooth.

3. Child like to play on swing.

4. A child is playing on our swing now.

5. I eat a lot of potato, bean, pea, and tomato.

6. I had a sandwich for lunch.

7. Some animal live in zoo.

8. Human have two foot.

9. The government of my country is a democracy.

10. Government collect tax.

► **Practice 5. Subjects, verbs, and objects.** (Chart 6-3)
Write "S" over the subject and "V" over the verb. If there is an object, write "O" over it.

          S   V   O
1. Caroline dropped a dish.

2. The dish fell.

3. The noise woke her baby.

4. The baby cried.

5. Caroline rocked her baby.

6. The phone rang.

7. A man came to the door.

8. The dog barked loudly.

9. Caroline answered the door.

► **Practice 6. Subjects, verbs, and objects.** (Chart 6-3)
Write the words in the lists in the correct order. Capitalize the first word in each sentence.
Write a **Ø** if there is no object.

1. children   play

Children	*play*	*Ø*
subject	verb	object of verb

2. children   ice cream   like

subject	verb	object of verb

3. a package   arrived   yesterday

subject	verb	object of verb

4. delivered   the mail carrier   the package

subject	verb	object of verb

5. my mother   the package   sent

subject	verb	object of verb

6. boarded   the airplane   the passengers

subject	verb	object of verb

7. left   the gate   the plane

subject	verb	object of verb

8. left   the plane   late

subject	verb	object of verb

► **Practice 7. Subjects, verbs, and objects.** (Chart 6-3)
Decide whether the word in **bold** is a noun or a verb. Write "N" for noun and "V" for verb above the word.

1. Andy hurt his **hand**.
   N

2. Students **hand** in homework assignments to their teachers.
   V

3. Ed has a loud **laugh**.

4. People always **laugh** at the comedian's jokes.

5. I usually **wash** my car on Saturday.

6. Maria put a big **wash** in the washing machine.

7. The Northeast got a lot of **snow** last night.

8. It's going to **snow** tomorrow.

9. The **text** is too small for me to read.

10. I **text** several friends every day.

11. Please **sign** your name on the dotted line.

12. The **sign** says *No left turn.*

► **Practice 8. Objects of prepositions.** (Chart 6-4)
Describe the picture. Complete the sentences with the correct prepositions.

1. The bird is (*in / on*) the cage.

2. The bird is standing (*in / on*) the bar.

3. The cage (*in / on*) the table.

4. The cat is (*beside / under*) the table.

5. The light is (*above / below*) the cat and the bird.

6. The bird and the cat are (*above / below*) the light.

7. The plant is (*behind / below*) the cage.

8. The cat is (*on / at*) the door of the cage.

9. The cat wants to go (*into / out*) the cage.

10. Maybe the bird will fly (*at / out*) of the cage.

▶ **Practice 9. Objects of prepositions.** (Chart 6-4)
Choose the correct completion from Column B.

Column A

1. The earth revolves ___.
2. The new office building is ___.
3. If you want an education, go ___.
4. A submarine travels ___.
5. If you are sick, stay ___.
6. The plane flew ___.

Column B

a. over the mountain
b. in bed
c. below the surface of the water
d. to college
e. between Fifth Avenue and Sixth Avenue
f. around the sun

Submarine

▶ **Practice 10. Prepositions.** (Chart 6-4)
Complete the sentences with the correct words from the lists.

in	into	near	of	on	to

1. A mosquito flew ____*in / into*____ the room from the patio. It didn't bother me because I had put insect repellent _____ my face and arms.
2. My checkbook is _____ the top drawer _____ my desk.
3. My home is not _____ my office. It takes me more than an hour to drive _____ my office every morning. That's a long drive.

above	below	from	of	on	through

4. The equator is an imaginary line that divides the earth in half. The Northern Hemisphere is _____ the equator, and the Southern Hemisphere is _____ the equator.

5. Europe is north _____ the equator.

6. Ecuador is a country in South America. It is called Ecuador—the Spanish word for equator—because the equator runs _____ the middle of it. When you look at a map, you see that Ecuador is _____ the equator.

7. Antarctica is very far south. It's far _____ the equator.

▶ **Practice 11. Objects of prepositions.** (Chart 6-4)

Part I. Read the passage. Circle the prepositions and underline the nouns that are objects of the prepositions.

A Hurricane in Jamaica

(1) We had a hurricane (in) Jamaica. Dark clouds appeared in the sky. Big waves rolled over the beaches. A strong wind blew through the trees. The rain fell hard on our roof. The water came under the door and into the house.

(2) After the storm, we walked around the neighborhood. Across the street, a tree was on the ground. Another tree was leaning against the house. Some electrical wires were hanging near the house too.

(3) The sun, which had been behind the clouds, finally appeared again. We were happy and grateful because we were standing beneath the hot Jamaican sun again.

Part II. Each statement is incorrect. Make true statements by correcting the prepositional phrases.

1. Dark clouds appeared through the trees.

   _____Dark clouds appeared in the sky._____

2. The water came in through the open window.

   _____

3. After the storm, the people walked outside the neighborhood.

   _____

4. The tree had fallen down on my house.

   _____

5. The sun had been in the clouds.

   _____

6. The neighbors felt happy and grateful when they were standing in the rain.

   _____

▶ **Practice 12. Prepositions of time.** (Chart 6-5)
Complete the sentences with *in*, *at*, or *on*.

The Jacksons got married . . .

1. _____*In*_____ the summer.
2. _____ June.
3. _____ June 17th.
4. _____ Saturday.
5. _____ 12:00 P.M.
6. _____ noon.
7. _____ 2007.
8. _____ Saturday afternoon.

Their baby was born . . .

9. _____ midnight.
10. _____ 12:00 A.M.
11. _____ the morning.
12. _____ April 12th.
13. _____ 2009.
14. _____ April.
15. _____ Wednesday.

▶ **Practice 13. Prepositions of time.** (Chart 6-5)
Complete the sentences with *in*, *at*, or *on*.

1. Jan is a nurse on the night shift. She works in the hospital _____ night. She sleeps _____ the morning. She does her errands _____ the afternoon. She works _____ weekends. She has her days off _____ Wednesdays and Thursdays.

2. Melissa is a new doctor at the hospital. She began work there _____ July 1st. _____ the present time, she is working in cardiology.* She is going to attend a lecture on cardiology _____ noon tomorrow. She is going to take an exam for cardiologists** _____ the summer. _____ the future, she wants to be a cardiologist.

▶ **Practice 14. Word order: place and time.** (Chart 6-6)
Complete the sentences. Use all the words in the list and the correct word order.

1. *to the airport, tomorrow morning*
   I'll take you _____.

2. *last month, a new job*
   Harry got _____.

3. *in January, in the mountains, skis*
   Our family always _____.

4. *at the coffee shop, in the morning, has breakfast*
   Gladys usually _____.

5. *last Sunday, jogged, in the park*
   We _____.

6. *bought, in the suburbs, last year, a house*
   The Green family _____.

---

cardiology = the medical study of the heart

**cardiologist* = a doctor who treats heart diseases

▶ **Practice 15. Word order: place and time.** (Chart 6-6)
Complete each sentence by putting the phrases in the correct order.

1. The police officer stopped   _1_ the driver.

                                  _2_ at a busy intersection.

                                  _3_ at midnight.

2. My friends rented   ____ on the lake.

                                 ____ last summer.

                                 ____ a sailboat.

3. The children caught   ____ in the river.

                                 ____ several fish.

                                 ____ last weekend.

4. We ate   ____ at noon.

                                 ____ our lunch.

                                 ____ in the park.

5. I bought   ____ a magazine.

                                 ____ at the corner newsstand.

                                 ____ after work yesterday.

▶ **Practice 16. Subject-verb agreement.** (Chart 6-7)
Complete the sentences with *is* or *are*.

1. These DVDs ___are___ from the library.

2. The DVDs from the library _____ past due.

3. Everyone _____ here.

4. Everybody _____ on time for class.

5. All the teachers _____ here.

6. Every teacher at this school _____ patient.

7. Some people _____ wise.

8. There _____ a good movie at the Sunset Theater this weekend.

9. There _____ some good movies in town over the weekend.

10. The rules of this game _____ easy.

11. This information about taxes _____ helpful.

▶ **Practice 17. Subject-verb agreement.** (Chart 6-7)
Choose the correct verb.

1. Bees (*make* / *makes*) honey.

2. Tomatoes (*needs* / *need*) lots of sunshine to grow.

3. (*Do* / *Does*) the people in your neighborhood help each other?

4. There (*is* / *are*) some people already in line for the movie.

5. The vegetables in the bowl on the table (*is* / *are*) fresh.

6. Everybody always (*comes* / *come*) to class on time.

7. Everyone in the class (*is* / *are*) paying attention.

8. The students in the class always (*pay* / *pays*) attention.

9. The dishes on the counter (*is* / *are*) dirty.

10. Every person (*needs* / *need*) to bring identification.

11. The people next door (*goes* / *go*) hiking every weekend in the summer.

12. My father and mother (*works* / *work*) for the same company.

13. The pictures on the wall (*is* / *are*) of my father's family.

▶ **Practice 18. Adjectives.** (Chart 6-8)
Underline each adjective. Draw an arrow to the noun it describes.

1. Paul has a loud voice.

2. Sugar is sweet.

3. The students took an easy test.

4. Air is free.

5. We ate some delicious food at a Mexican restaurant.

6. The child was sick.

7. The sick child got into his warm bed and sipped hot tea with honey and lemon in it.

▶ **Practice 19. Adjectives.** (Chart 6-8)
Complete each phrase with an adjective that has the opposite meaning.

1. new cars	_____old_____ cars	
2. a young man	an _____ man	
3. a good day	a _____ day	
4. hard exercises	_____ exercises	
5. a soft pillow	a _____ pillow	
6. a _____ street	a wide street	
7. _____ plates	dirty plates	
8. _____ cups	full cups	
9. dangerous cities	_____ cities	
10. a dark color	a _____ color	
11. a heavy box	a _____ box	
12. a _____ place	a private place	
13. my left foot	my _____ foot	
14. the wrong answer	the _____ answer	
15. a _____ walk	a short walk	

▶ **Practice 20. Using nouns as adjectives.** (Chart 6-9)
Use the information in *italics* to complete the sentences. Each completion should have a noun that is used as an adjective in front of another noun.

1. *Numbers on pages* are _____*page numbers*_____.

2. *Money that is made of paper* is _____.

3. *Buildings that have apartments* are _____.

4. *Gardens with roses* are _____.

5. *Chains for keys* are _____.

6. *Governments in cities* are _____.

7. *Walls made of bricks* are _____.

8. *Cartons that hold eggs* are _____.

9. *Views of mountains* are _____.

10. *Lights that control traffic* are _____.

11. *Pies that are made with apples* are _____.

12. *Bridges made from steel* are _____.

▶ **Practice 21. Using nouns as adjectives.** (Chart 6-9)
Choose the correct completion.

1. A: What kind of tree is that?
   B: It's a ____. It produces peaches in the summer.
   a. peaches tree   b. peach tree   c. tree peaches

2. A: So, you grew up on a farm. What kind of farm?
   B: A ____. We had chickens on the farm.
   a. farm chickens   b. chickens farm   c. chicken farm

3. A: We have a special dessert tonight. It's a cake made with carrots from the chef's own garden.
   B: Sounds good! I'll have the ____.
   a. carrot cake   b. carrots cake   c. cake carrots

4. A: What is a good present to get for your son? He likes to play games on the computer, right?
   B: Right. He loves ____.
   a. computers games   b. computer games   c. game computers

5. A: Are you going to travel in Canada by train?
   B: Yes, we are. We like ____.
   a. trip trains   b. train trips   c. trains trips

6. A: Look at that unusual building. Is it a new hotel?
   B: No. It's ____. A lot of big companies have their offices there.
   a. an office building   b. an offices building c. a building office

▶ **Practice 22. Adjectives.** (Charts 6-8 and 6-9)
Part I. Read the passage. It is adapted from a blog by astronaut Sandra Magnus. It was written from space in 2008.

The night sky below is not completely dark. The cloud cover over the earth reflects the city lights. There are lights above us too—white lights, red lights, and orange lights. They are all around us in space. They are everywhere. They sparkle.* You are swimming in a sea of beautiful lights. These bright lights in space are stars. You know that these shining stars are large, like our sun, and you know that they are very far from us. But from here, each star seems so tiny. You feel that space is enormous.**

Part II. Answer the questions according to the information in the passage. Circle "T" if the statement is true. Circle "F" if the statement is false.

1. Astronauts can see the earth's night sky from space.	T	F
2. The writer sees lights of different colors.	T	F
3. These lights are stars.	T	F
4. Each star looks small, but it is not really small.	T	F
5. The writer feels that space is tiny.	T	F

▶ **Practice 23. Review: nouns.** (Charts 6-1 → 6-9)
These sentences have mistakes in the use of nouns. Find each noun. Decide if the noun should be plural and add the correct plural form as necessary. Do not change any other words in the sentences.

1. The mountain ˢ in Chile are beautiful.

2. Cat hunt mouse.

3. Mosquito are small insect.

4. Everyone has eyelash.

---

*sparkle = shine in bright flashes

**enormous = very big in size or in amount

5. Do you listen to any podcasts when you take plane trip?

6. Forest sometimes have fire. Forest fire endanger wild animal.

7. Sharp kitchen knife can be dangerous.

8. I couldn't get concert tickets for Friday. The ticket were all sold out.

9. There are approximately 250,000 different kind of flower in the world.

10. I applied to several foreign university because I want to study in a different country.

11. Ted lives with three other university student.

12. In the past one hundred year, our daily life have changed in many way. We no longer need to
    use oil lamp or candle in our house, raise our own chicken, or build daily fire for cooking.

▶ **Practice 24. Personal pronouns: subjects and objects.** (Chart 6-10)
Underline the personal pronouns. Then write each pronoun and the noun it refers to.

1. Dr. Gupta is a math professor. Students like her very much. She makes them laugh.
   They enjoy Dr. Gupta's classes because they are fun.

   a. _____her_____ → _____Dr. Gupta_____

   b. _____ → _____

   c. _____ → _____

   d. _____ → _____

   e. _____ → _____

2. Dr. Reynolds is a dentist. Not many patients like him. He is not patient or gentle with them,
   but he is the only dentist in town, so many people go to him.

   a. _____ → _____

   b. _____ → _____

   c. _____ → _____

   d. _____ → _____

   e. _____ → _____

3. Beth says: "My hometown is a wonderful place. It's a small town. I know all the people there,
   and they know me. They are friendly. If you visit, they will welcome you."

   a. _____ → _____

   b. _____ → _____

   c. _____ → _____

   d. _____ → _____

   e. _____ → _____

   f. _____ → _____

   g. _____ → _____

   h. _____ → _____

► **Practice 25. Personal pronouns: subjects and objects.** (Chart 6-10)
Decide if the <u>underlined</u> word is a subject or object prounoun. Write "S" for subject and "O" for object above the underlined word.

                             O
1. Jackie just texted <u>me</u>.

     S
2. <u>She</u>'s going to be late.

3. Jia and Ning are arriving tomorrow. <u>They</u>'ll be here around noon.

4. Their parents will be happy to see <u>them</u>.

5. The doctor canceled the appointment. <u>He</u> has had an emergency.

6. If you need to speak to the doctor, call <u>him</u> tomorrow morning.

7. Bob and <u>I</u> had dinner last night.

8. <u>We</u> went to a restaurant on the lake.

9. George invited <u>us</u> to his wedding.

10. <u>It</u>'s going to be in June.

11. Your mother called and left a message. Call <u>her</u> right away.

12. Please answer <u>me</u> as soon as possible.

13. <u>You</u> live in the dorms, right?

14. See <u>you</u> tomorrow!

► **Practice 26. Personal pronouns: subjects and objects.** (Chart 6-10)
Check (✓) all the pronouns that can complete each sentence.

1. Mark called ＿＿＿ last night.

☐ he   ☐ her
☐ I   ☐ him
☐ me   ☐ she
☐ them   ☐ they
☐ us   ☐ we
☐ you

2. ＿＿＿ called Mark last night.

☐ He   ☐ Her
☐ Him   ☐ I
☐ Me   ☐ She
☐ Them   ☐ They
☐ Us   ☐ We
☐ You

3. Sharon saw ＿＿＿ on the plane.

☐ he and I   ☐ her and I
☐ him and me   ☐ him and I
☐ you and me   ☐ you and I
☐ she and I   ☐ she and me
☐ her and me   ☐ them and I
☐ they and me   ☐ them and us

4. ＿＿＿ saw Sharon on the plane.

☐ He and I   ☐ Her and I
☐ Him and me   ☐ Him and I
☐ You and me   ☐ You and I
☐ She and I   ☐ She and me
☐ Her and me   ☐ Them and I
☐ They and me   ☐ They and us

► **Practice 27. Personal pronouns.** (Chart 6-10)
Choose the correct pronoun.

1. Will you take (*I / me*) to the airport?

2. Will you take Jennifer and (*I / me*) to the airport?

3. Jennifer and (*I / me*) will be ready at 7:00 A.M.

4. Did you see Marta? *(She / Her)* was waiting in your office to talk to you.

5. I saw Ann a few minutes ago. I passed Sara, and (*she / her*) was talking to (*she / her*) in the hallway.

6. Nick used to work in his father's store, but his father and (*he / him*) had a serious disagreement. I think his father fired (*he / him*).

7. Prof. Molina called (*we / us*). He wants to see (*we / us*) in his office tomorrow morning.

8. Take these documents and destroy (*they / them*). (*They / Them*) contain personal and financial information.

► **Practice 28. Possessive nouns.** (Chart 6-11)
Choose the correct spelling of each possessive noun.

1. I have one cousin. My _____ name is Paul.
   a. cousin's   b. cousins'

2. I have two cousins. My _____ names are Paul and Kevin.
   a. cousin's   b. cousins'

3. I have three sons. My _____ names are Ryan, Jim, and Scott.
   a. son's   b. sons'

4. I have a son. My _____ name is Ryan.
   a. son's   b. sons'

5. I have a puppy. My _____ name is Rover.
   a. puppy's   b. puppies'

6. I have two puppies. My _____ names are Rover and Rex.
   a. puppie's   b. puppies'

7. I have one child. My _____ name is Anna.
   a. child's   b. childs'

8. I have two children. My _____ names are Anna and Keith.
   a. children's   b. childrens'

9. The winner of the dance contest was the judges' choice but not the _____ choice.
   a. people's   b. peoples'

10. Excuse me. Where is the _____ restroom?
    a. men's   b. mens'

▶ **Practice 29. Possessive nouns.** (Chart 6-11)
Write the possessive form of the *italicized* noun in the second sentence.

1. The book belongs to my *friend*. It's my _____friend's_____ book.

2. These books belong to my *friends*. They are my _____friends'_____ books.

3. The car belongs to my *parents*. It's my _____ car.

4. The car belongs to my *mother*. It's my _____ car.

5. This phone belongs to *Carl*. It's _____ phone.

6. The keys belong to *Carl*. They're _____ keys.

7. The toys belong to the *baby*. They are the _____ toys.

8. The toy belongs to the *baby*. It's the _____ toy.

9. The toys belong to the *babies*. They are the _____ toys.

10. This jacket belongs to *Ann*. It's _____ jacket.

11. The shoes belong to *Bob*. They are _____ shoes.

12. The shirt belongs to *James*. It's _____ shirt.

▶ **Practice 30. Possessive nouns.** (Chart 6-11)
Write the correct possessive form if necessary.

       Dan's
1. I met ~~Dan~~ sister yesterday.

2. I met Dan and his sister yesterday. (No change.)

3. I know Jack roommates.

4. I know Jack well. He's a good friend of mine.

5. I have one roommate. My roommate desk is always messy.

6. You have two roommates. Your roommates desks are always neat.

7. Jo Ann and Betty are sisters.

8. Jo Ann is Betty sister. My sister name is Sonya.

9. My name is Richard. I have two sisters. My sisters names are Jo Ann and Betty.

10. I read a book about the changes in women roles and men roles in modern society.

▶ **Practice 31. Possessive pronouns vs. possessive adjectives.** (Chart 6-12)
Complete the sentences with possessive pronouns or possessive adjectives that refer to the words in *italics*.

1. A: Can I look at your grammar book?
   B: Why? *You* have _____your_____ own* book. *You* have _____yours_____, and I have mine.

*****Own** frequently follows a possessive adjective: e.g., *my own, your own, their own*. The word **own** emphasizes that nobody else possesses the exact same thing(s); ownership belongs **only** to me (*my own book*), to you (*your own book*), to them (*their own books*), to us (*our own books*), etc.

2. A: Kim wants to look at your grammar book.
   B: Why? *She* has _____ own book. *She* has _____, and I have mine.

3. A: Jake wants to look at your grammar book.
   B: Why? *He* has _____ own book. *He* has _____, and I have mine.

4. A: Jake and I want to look at your grammar book.
   B: Why? *You* have _____ own books. *You* have _____, and I have mine.

5. A: Jake and Kim want to look at our grammar books.
   B: Why? *They* have _____ own books. *We* have _____ own books. *They* have _____, and *we* have _____.

▶ **Practice 32. Possessive pronouns vs. possessive adjectives.** (Chart 6-12)
Choose the correct word.

1. *Mrs. Lee* asked (*her* / *hers*) kids to clean up the kitchen.

2. I don't need to borrow your bicycle. *My sister* lent me (*her* / *hers*).

3. *Ted and I* are roommates. (*Our* / *Ours*) apartment is small.

4. *Brian and Louie* have a bigger apartment. In fact, (*their* / *theirs*) is huge.

5. *You* can find (*your* / *yours*) keys in the top drawer of the desk.

6. The keys in the drawer belong to you. *I* have (*my* / *mine*) in (*my* / *mine*) pocket. *You* should look in the drawer for (*your* / *yours*).

7. *Tom and Paul* talked about (*their* / *theirs*) experiences in the wilderness areas of Canada. I've had a lot of interesting experiences in the wilderness, but nothing to compare with (*their* / *theirs*).

8. *I* know Eric well. He is a good friend of (*my* / *mine*). *You* know him too, don't you? Isn't he a friend of (*you* / *yours*) too?

▶ **Practice 33. Reflexive pronouns.** (Chart 6-13)
Complete the sentences with reflexive pronouns that refer to the words in *italics*.

1. *I* enjoyed _____myself_____ at Disney World.

2. *We* all enjoyed _____ there.

3. *Uncle Joe* enjoyed _____.

4. *Aunt Elsa* enjoyed _____.

5. *Jessica and Paul* enjoyed _____.

6. Hi, Emily! Did *you* enjoy _____?

7. Hi, Emily and Dan! Did *you* enjoy _____?

8. In its advertising, *Disney World* calls _____ "the happiest place in the world."

Complete each sentence with an appropriate expression from the list. Be sure to use the correct reflexive pronoun.

be proud of	✓cut	help	take care of	teach
blame	enjoy	introduce	talk to	work for

1. Ouch! I just _____*cut myself*_____ with a knife.

2. You got a scholarship to State College? Congratulations, Anna! You must _____
   _____ .

3. John often _____ . People think there is more than one person
   in the room, but there isn't. It's only John.

4. When I was young, I _____ to ride a bicycle. Then I taught the
   other children in the neighborhood.

5. Sheri _____ for the accident, but it wasn't her fault. The other
   car didn't stop at the stop sign and crashed into hers.

6. Eat, eat! There's lots more pizza in the oven. Please, all of you, _____
   _____ to more pizza.

7. Adam seldom gets sick because he eats healthy food and exercises regularly. He _____
   _____ .

8. They went to a party last night. Let's ask them if they _____ .

9. My father never worked for anyone. He always owned his own company. He
   _____ throughout his entire adult life.

10. At the beginning of each term, my students _____ to the whole class.

▶ **Practice 35. Review: pronouns and possessive adjectives.** (Charts 6-10 → 6-13)
Choose the correct pronouns.

1. Alan invited (*I* / ⓜⓔ) to go to dinner with (*he* / ⓗⓘⓜ).

2. Sam and you should be proud of (*yourself* / *yourselves*). The two of you did a good job.

3. The room was almost empty. The only furniture was one table. The table stood by (*it* / *itself*)
   in one corner.

4. The bird returned to (*its* / *it's*★) nest to feed (*its* / *it's*) baby bird.

5. Nick has his tennis racket, and Ann has (*her* / *hers* / *her's*★).

6. Where's Eric? I have some good news for Joe and (*he* / *him* / *his* / *himself*).

7. Don't listen to Greg. You need to think for (*yourself* / *yourselves*), Jane. It's
   (*you* / *your* / *your's*★) life.

8. We all have (*us* / *our* / *ours*) own ideas about how to live (*our* / *ours* / *our's*★) lives.

★REMINDER: Apostrophes are NOT used with possessive pronouns. Note that *its* = possessive adjective; *it's* = *it is*. Also note that *her's, your's,* and *our's* are NOT POSSIBLE in grammatically correct English.

9. You have your beliefs, and we have (*our / ours*).

10. People usually enjoy (*themselves / theirselves**) at family gatherings.

11. History repeats (*himself / herself / itself*).

12. David didn't need my help. He finished the work by (*him / himself / hisself*).

▶ **Practice 36. Review: pronouns and possessive adjectives.** (Charts 6-10 → 6-13)
Complete each passage with words from the list. You may use a word more than once. Capitalize words as necessary.

> he   him   himself   his

(1) Tom is wearing a bandage on _____*his*_____ arm. _____*He*_____ hurt _____*himself*_____
      while _____ was repairing the roof. I'll help _____ with the
                            4   5
    roof later.

> her   I   mine   she
> hers   it   our   we

(2) I have a sister. _____ name is Katherine, but we call _____
                                      1   2
    Kate. _____ and I share a room. _____ room is pretty small.
                    3   4
    _____ have only one desk. _____ has five drawers. Kate puts
            5   6
    _____ things in the two drawers on the right. I keep _____ in
            7   8
    the two drawers on the left. Kate doesn't open my two drawers, and I don't open
    _____. She and _____ share the middle drawer.
            9   10

> he   his   their   them   they
> her   my   theirs   themselves

(3) Mr. Ramirez is the manager of our office. _____ has a corner office with
                                                              1
    _____ name on the door. Ms. Lake is _____ assistant.
            2   3
    _____ office is next to Mr. Ramirez's office. _____ often work
            4   5
    together on projects by _____, but I work with _____
                                      6   7
    sometimes. They never come to _____ office to meet. I always go to
                                                  8
    _____. I take an elevator to get to _____ offices, or I walk up a
            9   10
    long flight of stairs.

---

*NOTE: *Themself* and *theirselves* are not really words—they are NOT POSSIBLE in grammatically correct English. Only ***themselves*** is the correct reflexive pronoun form.

▶ **Practice 37. Singular forms of *other*: *another* vs. *the other.*** (Chart 6-14)
Write *another* or *the other* under each picture.

1. four boxes: ___one___   ___another___   ___another___   ___the other___

2. three circles: ___one___   _____   _____

3. five flowers: ___one___   _____   _____   _____   _____

4. two cups: ___one___   _____

5. six spoons: ___one___   _____   _____   _____   _____   _____

▶ **Practice 38. Singular forms of *other*: *another* vs. *the other.*** (Chart 6-14)
Complete the sentences with *another* or *the other*.

1. There are two girls in Picture A. One is Ann. _____ is Sara.

PICTURE A

ANN   SARA

PICTURE B

ALEX   MIKE   DAVID

2. There are three boys in Picture B. One is Alex. _____ one is Mike.

3. In Picture B, Alex and Mike are smiling. _____ boy looks sad.

4. There are three boys in Picture B. All three have common first names. One is named Alex.

    a. _____ is named David.

    b. The name of _____ one is Mike.

5. There are many common English names for boys. Alex is one.

    a. Mike is _____ .

    b. David is _____ .

    c. John is _____ common name.

    d. Joe is _____ .

    e. What is _____ common English name for a boy?

▶ **Practice 39. Plural forms of *other*: *other(s)* vs. *the other(s)*.** (Chart 6-15)
Complete the sentences with ***the other***, ***the others***, ***other***, or ***others***.

1. There are four common nicknames for "Robert." One is "Bob." Another is "Bobby."

    _____<u>The others</u>_____ are "Robbie" and "Rob."

2. There are five English vowels. One is "a." Another is "e." _____ are "i,"
"o," and "u."

3. There are many consonants in English. The letters "b" and "c" are consonants.

    _____ are "d," "f," and "g."

4. Some people are tall, and _____ are short. Some people are neither tall

    nor short.

5. Some people are tall, and _____ people are short.

6. Some animals are huge. _____ are tiny.

7. Some animals are huge. _____ animals are tiny.

8. Of the twenty students in the class, eighteen passed the exam. _____

    failed.

9. Out of the twenty students in the class, only two failed the exam. _____

    students passed.

▶ **Practice 40. Summary: forms of *other*.** (Charts 6-14 → 6-16)
Choose the correct completion.

1. Gold is one kind of metal. Silver is ____.
    a. another   b. the other   c. the others   d. others   e. other

2. Summer is one season. Spring is ____.
    a. another   b. the other   c. the others   d. others   e. other

3. There are four seasons. Summer is one. ____ are winter, fall, and spring.
    a. Another   b. The other   c. The others   d. Others   e. Other

4. What's your favorite season? Some people like spring the best. ____ think fall is the nicest
season.
    a. Another   b. The other   c. The others   d. Others   e. Other

5. This cat's eyes are different colors. One eye is gray, and ____ is green.
    a. another   b. the other   c. the others   d. others   e. other

6. There are two reasons not to buy that piece of furniture. One is that it's expensive. _____ is that it's not well made.
   a. Another   b. The other   c. The others   d. Others   e. Other

7. Alex failed his English exam, but his teacher is going to give him _____ chance to pass it.
   a. another   b. the other   c. the others   d. others   e. other

8. Some people drink tea in the morning. _____ have coffee. I prefer fruit juice.
   a. Another   b. The other   c. The others   d. Others   e. Other

9. There are five digits in the number 20,000. One digit is a 2. _____ digits are all zeroes.
   a. Another   b. The other   c. The others   d. Others   e. Other

▶ **Practice 41. Review.** (Chapter 6)
Choose the correct completion.

1. The people at the market (*is* / *are*) friendly.

2. How many (*potato* / *potatoes*) should I cook for dinner tonight?

3. I wanted to be alone, so I worked (*myself* / *by myself*).

4. The twins were born (*in* / *on*) December 25th (*on* / *at*) midnight.

5. On the small island, there are seven (*vacation* / *vacations*) houses.

6. The bus driver waited for (*we* / *us*) at the bus stop.

7. Can you tell a good book by (*its* / *it's*) title?

8. This is (*our* / *ours*) dessert, and that is (*your* / *yours*).

9. Jack has so much confidence. He really believes in (*him* / *himself*).

10. These bananas are okay, but (*the other* / *the others*) were better.

▶ **Practice 42. Editing.** (Chapter 6)
Correct the errors.

1. Look at those beautifuls mountains!

2. The children played on Saturday afternoon at the park a game.

3. There are two horse, several sheeps, and a cow in the farmers field.

4. The owner of the store is busy in the moment.

5. The teacher met her's students at the park after school.

6. Everyone want peace in the world.

7. I grew up in a city very large.

8. This apple tastes sour. There are more, so let's try the other one.

9. Some tree lose their leaf in the winter.

10. I am going to wear my shirt blue to the party.

11. People may hurt theirselves if they use this machine.

12. Our neighbors invited my friend and I to visit they.

13. My husband boss works for twelve hour every days.

14. The students couldn't find they're books.

15. I always read magazines articles while I'm in the waiting room at my dentists office.

▶ **Practice 43. Word search puzzle.**
Circle the plural forms of the these words in the puzzle: *man, woman, child, tooth, fly, foot, fox, wolf, monkey*. The words may be horizontal, vertical, or diagonal. The first letter of each word is highlighted in gray.

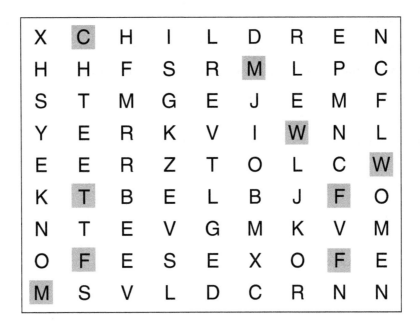

Chapter 7
Modal Auxiliaries

▶ **Practice 1. The form of modal auxiliaries.** (Chart 7-1)

Add the word **to** where necessary. Write **Ø** if **to** is not necessary.

1. Mr. Alvarez spilled ketchup on his shirt. He must ___Ø___ change clothes before dinner.

2. Mr. Alvarez has ___to___ change his shirt before dinner.

3. Tom and I might _____ play soccer after work tomorrow.

4. Would you _____ speak more slowly, please?

5. The students have _____ take a test next Friday.

6. Everyone should _____ wash their hands before meals.

7. Everyone ought _____ cover their mouth when they cough.*

8. May I please _____ have the salt and pepper? Thanks.

9. You'd better not _____ come to the meeting late. The boss will _____ be angry if you're late.

10. I've been going to bed after midnight. The next day, I can't _____ stay awake in class. I've got _____ go to bed earlier from now on.

11. With that cough, you had better _____ see a doctor soon. I think you may have _____ pneumonia.**

▶ **Practice 2. Expressing ability.** (Chart 7-2)

Complete each sentence with the correct word in parentheses. Note the words in **boldface**.

1. (*giraffe, zebra*)   A ___zebra___ **can't stretch** its neck to reach the tops of trees.

2. (*bee, cat*)   A single _____ **can kill** a thousand mice in a year.

3. (*Rabbits, Elephants*)   _____ **can break** small trees under their huge feet.

4. (*Monkeys, Chickens*)   _____ **can climb** trees easily.

5. (*ducks, camels*)   Did you know that _____ **can survive** 17 days without any water at all?

6. (*cow, bull*)   One _____ **can produce** as much as 8,500 lbs. (3,860 kgs) of milk in a year.

7. (*horse, cat*)   A person **can sit** on a _____ without hurting it.

---

*cough = a sudden push of air out of your throat with a shout sound.

**pneumonia = a serious illness that affects your lungs and makes it difficult for you to breathe.

8. (*donkey, snake*) A _____ **can carry** heavy loads on its back.

9. (*squirrel, polar bear*) A _____ **can stay** high up in the trees for weeks and jump from branch to branch.

10. (*people, ants*) Most _____ **can lift** objects that are ten times heavier than their own bodies.

▶ **Practice 3. Expressing possibility and permission.** (Chart 7-3)
Decide if the meaning of the modal verb is *possibility* or *permission*.

Meaning

1. Both of my grandparents are retired. They like to travel. They **may travel** overseas next summer. (possibility)   permission

2. They **may take** their two grandchildren with them.   possibility   permission

3. A: Yes, Tommy, you **may play** outdoors until dinner.
   B: Okay, Mom.   possibility   permission

4. A: What's wrong with the dog's foot?
   B: He **may have** an infection.   possibility   permission

5. The dog has an infected foot. He **might need** to go to the vet.   possibility   permission

6. A: I'm sorry, sir, but passengers **can't walk** around the plane when the "Fasten seat belt sign" is on.
   B: Oh, okay. I'm sorry.   possibility   permission

7. It **may be** hot and humid all weekend.   possibility   permission

8. If you finish the test early, you **may** leave.   possibility   permission

9. I **might not stay** up to watch the end of the game on TV. I'm very sleepy.   possibility   permission

10. A: Excuse me. **Can I ask** you a personal question?
    B: Hmmm . . . I don't know about that. I really don't like personal questions.   possibility   permission

▶ **Practice 4. Expressing possibility.** (Chart 7-3)
Rewrite each sentence using the word in parentheses.

1. Maybe I will take a nap. (*might*) _____*I might take a nap.*_____

2. She might be sick. (*maybe*) _____*Maybe she is sick.*_____

3. There may be time later. (*maybe*) _____

4. Maybe our team will win. (*may*) _____

5. You may be right. (*might*) _____

6. Maybe we'll hear soon. (*may*) _____

7. It might rain. (*may*) _____

8. Maybe it will snow. (*might*) _____

9. She might come tomorrow. (*maybe*) _____

10. She might be at home right now. (*maybe*) _____

Choose the correct completion.

1. A: Are you running in the big race tomorrow, Alan?
    B: No, I'm not. I _____ run. I broke my foot on Saturday and now it's in a cast.
    a. can   c. may
    b. can't   d. may not

2. A: Where's Tracy? I've been looking for her all morning.
    B: I haven't seen her. She _____ be sick.
    a. can   c. might
    b. can't   d. might not

3. A: I heard that Jessica has gotten a scholarship to Duke University!
    B: It's not definite yet, but she _____ get one. The admissions office says that it's possible and they will let us know next month.
    a. can   c. might
    b. can't   d. might not

4. A: Larry has been in New York for a couple of months. Is he going to stay there or return home?
    B: It depends. If he _____ find a job there soon, he'll stay. If not, he'll come home.
    a. can   c. may
    b. can't   d. may not

5. A: Is Jodie a doctor now?
    B: Not yet, but almost. She finished medical school last month, but she hasn't taken her exams yet. She _____ be a doctor until she passes them.
    a. can   c. might
    b. can't   d. might not

6. A: When are you going to sell your old car?
    B: As soon as I _____ find someone to buy it!
    a. can   c. may
    b. can't   d. may not

► **Practice 6. Meanings of *could*.** (Charts 7-2 and 7-4)
Choose the expression that has the same meaning as the *italicized* verb.

1. A: How long will it take you to paint two small rooms?
    B: I'm not sure. If the job is not complicated, I *could finish* by Thursday.
    a. was able to finish   b. might finish

2. I think I'll take my umbrella. It *could rain* today.
    a. was able to rain   b. might rain

3. My niece *could read* by the time she was four years old.
    a. was able to read   b. might read

4. You *could see* that the little boy was unhappy because of the sad expression in his eyes.
    a. were able to see   b. might see

5. Sally is in excellent condition. I think she *could win* the 10-kilometer race on Saturday.
    a. was able to win   b. might win

6. John *couldn't drive* for a month because of a broken ankle, but now it's healed.
   a. wasn't able to drive   b. might not drive

7. Jane *could arrive* before dinner, but I don't really expect her until nine or later.
   a. was able to arrive   b. might arrive

8. Simon was in an accident, but he *couldn't remember* how he had hurt himself.
   a. wasn't able to remember   b. might not remember

▶ **Practice 7. Polite questions: *May I, Could I, Can I.*** (Chart 7-5)
Complete the conversations. Write the letter of the question that matches each answer.

```
a. Can I borrow the book when you finish it?
b. Could I pick you up at 6:30 instead of 6:00?
c. Could we watch the comedy instead of the war movie?
d. May I ask you a question?
e. May I have some more potatoes, please?
f. May I help you?
```

1. A: _____
   B: Yes. They're delicious, aren't they?

2. A: _____
   B: Yes. What would you like to know?

3. A: _____
   B: Thanks. I want to buy this.

4. A: _____
   B: That's a little late.

5. A: _____
   B: Sure. I'm in the mood for something funny.

6. A: _____
   B: Yes. I'll probably finish it tonight.

▶ **Practice 8. Polite questions.** (Charts 7-5 and 7-6)
Complete each part of the conversation with the correct word from the list. More than one word may be correct.

(1) *may, would*

A: Hello, Tracy Johnson's office. _____ I help you?
                                          1

B: Yes, please. I'd like to speak to Ms. Johnson.

A: I'm sorry. She's in a meeting. _____ you leave your name and number? I'll
                                          2
   ask her to call you back.

B: Yes. It's 555-7981.

A: _____ I ask what this is about?
          3

B: Well, I have some good news for her. _____ you please tell her that?
                                                  4

(2) *will, could*

A: Of course.

B: And _____ you please tell her that this is important?
         5

A: All right, I certainly will. _____ I ask you just one more thing?
                                    6

B: Yes?

A: _____ you please leave me your name? You forgot to tell me that.
      7

▶ **Practice 9. Polite questions.** (Charts 7-5 and 7-6)
Check (✓) all the modal auxiliaries that correctly complete each question.

1. It's cold in here. ___ you please close the door?
   ___ May   ✓ Could   ✓ Can   ✓ Would

2. Oh, I forgot my wallet. ___ I borrow ten dollars from you until tomorrow?
   ___ Could   ___ May   ___ Will   ___ Can

3. I can't lift this box by myself. ___ you help me carry it?
   ___ Would   ___ Could   ___ May   ___ Will

4. Hello. ___ I help you find something in the store?
   ___ Can   ___ Would   ___ May   ___ Could

5. The store closes in ten minutes. ___ you please bring all your purchases to the counter?
   ___ Will   ___ May   ___ Can   ___ Could

▶ **Practice 10. Expressing advice.** (Chart 7-7)
Complete the sentences. Use *should* or *shouldn't* and the expressions in the list.

always be on time for an appointment	drive the speed limit
attend all classes	give too much homework
be cruel to animals	quit
✓ drive a long distance	throw trash out of your car window

1. If you are tired, you ___*shouldn't drive a long distance*___.

2. Cigarette smoking is dangerous to your health. You _____.

3. A good driver _____.

4. A teacher _____.

5. A student _____.

6. Animals have feelings. You _____.

7. It is important to be punctual. You _____

   _____.

8. Littering is against the law. You _____
_____.

▶ **Practice 11. Expressing advice.** (Chart 7-7)
Write the letter of the word or phrase that correctly completes each sentence.

a. ask her again	f. read the instructions first
b. eat it	g. stick to my diet
c. find a new girl friend	h. study
d. go to the game	i. wash it in cold water
e. keep pushing all the buttons	j. wash it in hot water

1. A: Should I wash this sweater in hot water to get the spot out?

    B: No. You shouldn't _____. The sweater will shrink if you wash it in hot water. You should _____.

2. A: This is my new TV remote,* but I can't figure out how to use it.

    B: You shouldn't _____. You should _____.

3. A: You like this chocolate cake, don't you?

    B: I love it, but I shouldn't _____. I'm trying to lose weight. I should _____.

4. A: Are you going to study for the exam tonight?

    B: I should _____, but I'm not going to. I'm going to the basketball game.

    A: How come?

    B: Well, I shouldn't _____, but I really want to see it. Our team might win the championship tonight!

5. A: I have asked Linda to marry me five times. She always says "No." What should I do? Should I ask her again?

    B: No, of course not! You shouldn't _____. You should _____.

_____

*remote = remote control

Choose the correct completion.

1. Danny doesn't feel well. He _____ see a doctor.
   (a.) should   b. ought   c. had

2. Danny doesn't feel well. He _____ better see a doctor.
   a. should   b. ought   c. had

3. Danny doesn't feel well. He _____ to see a doctor.
   a. should   b. ought   c. had

4. It's very warm in here. We _____ open some windows.
   a. should   b. ought   c. had

5. It's really cold in here. We _____ to close some windows.
   a. should   b. ought   c. had

6. There's a police car behind us. You _____ better slow down!
   a. should   b. ought   c. had

7. People who use public parks _____ clean up after themselves.
   a. should   b. ought   c. had

8. I have no money left in my bank account. I _____ better stop charging things on my credit card.
   a. should   b. ought   c. had

9. It's going to be a formal dinner and dance. You _____ to change clothes.
   a. should   b. ought   c. had

10. This library book is overdue. I _____ better return it today.
    a. should   b. ought   c. had

▶ **Practice 13. Expressing necessity.** (Chart 7-9)
Read the passage. Complete each sentence with a word from the list.

have	has	had	must

Applying to College

I'm applying to colleges now. I would like to go to Stellar University, but they probably won't accept me. First, students _____ to have excellent grades to go there, and my grades
                                      1
are only average. Second, a student _____ be in the top 10 percent of the class, and
                                      2
I am not. I am in the top 30 percent. Third, everybody _____ to take a difficult
                                                          3
examination and do well on it. I am not good at examinations. I _____ to take
                                                                  4
many examinations when I was younger, and I didn't do well on any of them.

On the other hand, I think they will accept me at People's University. First, at this school, a student doesn't _____ to have excellent grades, just good ones. Second, there is no
5
entrance examination. Instead, you just _____ to write a couple of good essays, and
6
I am good at writing. I _____ to write a lot of compositions last year, and I always
7
did well.

You _____ got to be realistic when you choose your university. I think I am very
8
realistic and I expect People's University will be a good fit for me.

▶ **Practice 14. Necessity: _must, have to, have got to._** (Chart 7-9)
Choose the correct verb.

1. Last week, John (*had to / must*) interview five people for the new management position.
2. Professor Drake (*had got to / had to*) cancel several lectures when she became ill.
3. Why did you (*have to / had to*) leave work early?
4. I (*must / had to*) take my daughter to the airport yesterday.
5. Where did John (*have to / had to*) go for medical help yesterday?
6. We (*had to / had got to*) contact a lawyer last week about a problem with our neighbors.
7. I (*have got to / had to*) leave now. I (*have to / had to*) pick up my kids. They're waiting at school.
8. You (*had to / must*) have a pencil with an eraser for the exam. Do not bring a pen.

▶ **Practice 15. Necessity: _must, have to, have got to._** (Chart 7-9)
Write the past tense of the verbs in *italics*.

1. I *have to study* for my medical school exams.

    PAST: I _____*had to study*_____ for my medical school exams.

2. We *have to turn off* our water because of a leak.

    PAST: We _____ our water because of a leak.

3. *Do* you *have to work* over the holidays?

    PAST: _____ you _____ over the holidays?

4. Jerry *has got to see* the dentist twice this week.

    PAST: Jerry _____ the dentist twice last month.

5. Who *has got to be* in early for work this week?

    PAST: Who _____ in early for work last week?

6. The bank *must close* early today.

    PAST: The bank _____ early yesterday.

▶ **Practice 16. Expressing necessity.** (Chart 7-9)
Check (✓) the sentence that best completes each conversation.

1. A: Ma'am, show me your driver's license, please.
   B: Of course, officer. But what did I do? Why did you pull me over?
   A: ☐ You didn't stop at the red light. You have to stop at red lights.
      ☐ You've got to be on time for work.
      ☐ You have to fill out this form.

2. A: Son, what happened? You didn't call to say that you were going to be late.
   B: I'm sorry. I forgot.
   A: ☐ You must get better grades.
      ☐ You have to clean up your room.
      ☐ You've got to be more responsible.

3. A: Nice shoes. But they're big for you!
   B: Well, I ordered them from an Internet site, but they sent the wrong ones instead.
   A: ☐ You must wear better shoes.
      ☐ You've got to walk a lot.
      ☐ You have to send them back and get the right ones.

4. A: May I help you?
   B: Yes. I'm here to apply for the assistant teacher's job.
   A: ☐ Okay. Everyone has to apply for a job.
      ☐ Okay. Everyone must fill out an application. Here it is.
      ☐ Okay. Everyone has got to pay attention.

5. A: Ms. Honeywell, Jimmy will be better in a few days.
   B: Should he take any medicine, doctor?
   A: ☐ No. He has got to play football tomorrow.
      ☐ No. He has to take this medicine three times a day.
      ☐ No. He just has to stay in bed for a couple of days and drink plenty of water.

▶ **Practice 17. Expressing lack of necessity and prohibition.** (Chart 7-10)
Complete the sentences with **don't have to** or **must/must not**.

1. To fly from one country to another, you _____ must _____ have a plane ticket and a passport.

2. To fly from one city to another in the same country, it's necessary to have a plane ticket, but you _____ have a passport.

3. Billy, you are allergic to bees. There are a lot of bees in the flowers. You _____ play near them.

4. You _____ order fish in this seafood restaurant. You can have chicken or beef if you prefer.

5. Because you are feeling better, you _____ take this medicine.

6. Susie, you _____ take this medicine. It's for adults, not children. It will make you sick.

7. If you see a sign that says "No Left Turn," you _____ turn left there.

8. When your phone rings, you _____ answer it. The caller can leave a message.

9. When you are in a theater, you _____ use your cell phone. You have to turn it off.

10. It's warm all the time in Hawaii, so you _____ wear heavy sweaters and jackets there.

11. The wedding is very formal. Everyone has to wear formal clothes. You _____ wear jeans or sandals.

▶ **Practice 18. Expressing necessity, lack of necessity, and prohibition.**
(Charts 7-9 and 7-10)
Write the phrases in the correct columns.

cook every meal themselves   say "sir" or "madam" to others drive without a license   stay in their homes in the evening eat and drink in order to live   stop when they see a police car's lights behind them ✓fall asleep while driving   take other people's belongings pay taxes

People have to / must . . . (necessary)	People must not . . . (Don't!)	People don't have to . . . (not necessary)
	fall asleep while driving	

► **Practice 19. Logical conclusions.** (Chart 7-11)
Write the letter of the sentence in Column B that correctly describes the sentence in Column A.

Five Cousins at the Dinner Table

Column A

1. Isabel has eaten two potatoes and now she is asking for another one. _____

2. Rose is sitting at the table, but she isn't eating anything. She had a dish of ice cream just before dinner. _____

3. Emlly is telling everyone about her trip to Costa Rica. She is leaving next week. _____

4. Jill just tasted some fish and made a funny face. _____

5. Natalie has fallen asleep at the dinner table! _____

Column B

a. She must not like it.

b. She must be very tired.

c. She must like them.

d. She must not be hungry.

e. She must be excited about it.

► **Practice 20. Logical conclusion or necessity.** (Charts 7-9 and 7-11)
Write "1" if *must* expresses a logical conclusion. Write "2" if *must* expresses necessity.

1 = **logical conclusion**
2 = **necessity**

1. _____2_____ You *must have* a passport to travel abroad.
2. _____1_____ You *must like* to read. You have such a large library.
3. _____ You *must take off* your shoes before entering this room.
4. _____ The dessert *must be* good. It's almost gone.
5. _____ You *must try* this dessert. It's wonderful.
6. _____ Children *must stay* seated during the flight.
7. _____ You *must pay* in advance if you want a front-row seat for the performance.
8. _____ Ellen *must* really *like* being at the beach. She goes there every vacation.

► **Practice 21. Tag questions with modal auxiliaries.** (Chart 7-12)
Complete the tag questions with the correct modal auxiliary.

1. You won't tell anyone, _____ you?

2. George can help us, _____ he?

3. Mr. Cheng would like to come with us, _____ he?

4. You would rather stay home, _____ you?

5. Sally can't speak French, _____ she?

6. You don't have to work next weekend, _____ you?

7. Teachers shouldn't give too much homework, _____ they?

8. I'll see you tomorrow, _____ I?

9. You couldn't hear me, _____ you?

10. We should cross the street here, _____ we?

11. Ms. Scott has to take a driving course, _____ she?

12. If Grandma is expecting us at 6:00, we should leave here at 4:00, _____ we?

▶ **Practice 22. Giving instructions: imperative sentences.** (Chart 7-13)
Pretend that someone says the following sentences to you. Which verbs give instructions?
<u>Underline</u> the imperative verbs.

1. I'll be right back. <u>Wait</u> here.

2. <u>Don't wait</u> for Rebecca. She's not going to come.

3. Read pages 39 to 55 before class tomorrow.

4. What are you doing? Don't put those magazines in the trash. I haven't read them yet.

5. Come in and have a seat. I'll be right with you.

DON'T CROSS THIS
FIELD UNLESS YOU
CAN DO IT IN
9.9 SECONDS.
THE BULL CAN
DO IT IN 10.
(NO TRESPASSING)

▶ **Practice 23. Polite questions and imperatives.** (Charts 7-5, 7-6, and 7-13)
Number the sentences in each group in order of politeness. "1" is the **most polite**.

1. _1_ Could you open the door?

    _3_ Open the door.

    _2_ Can you open the door?

2. ____ Get the phone, please.

   ____ Would you please get the phone?

   ____ Get the phone.

   ____ Can you get the phone?

3. ____ Hand me the calculator.

   ____ Will you hand me the calculator, please?

   ____ Would you hand me the calculator, please?

   ____ Please hand me the calculator.

► **Practice 24. *Let's and Why don't.*** (Chart 7-14)
Complete the conversation with verbs from the lists.

Six Neighborhood Friends

Six neighborhood friends have grown up together. They are very close. They meet for breakfast on Sundays and then try to do something active together during the day. Here's a conversation they had on one recent Sunday.

Part I. *fly, listen, sail, walk*

JOHNNY: There's a strong wind today. Let's _____ our kites on the beach today.
              ₁

BOBBY: No, the wind is perfect for sailing. Let's _____ on the lake today. We could
              ₂

rent two boats for a few hours.

GRACE: Why don't we _____ over to the park? It's a beautiful day, and we could have a
              ₃

great time. There's a country music festival there today.

DORA: Yes, let's go to the park and _____ to country music.
              ₄

Part II. *go, see, shop*

ALICE: I don't like country music very much. I'd rather go to the mall. Let's _____
              ₅

shopping. They're having a big holiday sale today.

TIMMY: Shopping is boring. I'll tell you what. Alice, why don't you _____ and the rest
              ₆

of us will do something else.

ALICE: Hmmm. Grace, do you want to drive over to the mall with me?

GRACE: No, I'd rather do something as a group. Okay, guys—let's _____. What can
              ₇

the rest of us enjoy as a group?

Part III. *do, have, plan, tell*

JOHNNY: I think we should go to the country music festival together. They have a lot of great

musicians. After that, let's _____ pizza at my house. We can order it from the
              ₈

Pizza Pan.

BOBBY: Okay. Let's _____ that today—go to the festival and end up at Johnny's. Then
              ₉

let's _____ a sailing day next week. Johnny, why don't you _____
        ₁₀   ₁₁

your parents we're having a pizza dinner and invite them to join us too?

▶ **Practice 25. Stating preferences.** (Chart 7-15)
Complete the sentences with *prefer*, *like(s)*, or *would rather*.

1. I ____*prefer*____ cold weather to hot weather.

2. A: What's your favorite fruit?
   B: I ____*like*____ strawberries better than any other fruit.

3. Mary ____*would rather*____ save money than enjoy herself.

4. A: Why isn't your brother going with us to the movie?
   B: He _____ stay home and read than go out on a Saturday night.

5. A: Does Peter _____ football to baseball?
   B: No. I think he _____ baseball better than football.
   A: Then why didn't he go to the game yesterday?
   B: Because he _____ watch sports on TV than go to a ball park.

6. A: Do you want to go out to the Japanese restaurant for dinner?
   B: That would be okay, but in truth I _____ Chinese food to
      Japanese food.
   A: Really? I _____ Japanese food better than Chinese food. What
      shall we do?
   B: Let's go to the Italian restaurant.

▶ **Practice 26. Stating preferences.** (Chart 7-15)
Use the words in parentheses to make a new sentence with the same meaning.

1. Alex would rather swim than jog. (*prefer*)
   ____*Alex prefers swimming to jogging.*____

2. My son would rather eat fish than beef. (*would rather*)
   _____

3. Kim likes salad better than dessert. (*prefer*)
   _____

4. In general, Nicole would rather have coffee than tea. (*like*)
   _____

5. Bill prefers teaching history to working as a business executive. (*would rather*)
   _____

6. When considering a pet, Sam prefers dogs to cats. (*like*)
   _____

7. On a long trip, Susie would rather drive than ride in the back seat. (*prefer*)
   _____

8. I like studying in a noisy room better than studying in a quiet room. (*would rather*)
   _____

9. Alex likes soccer better than baseball. (*would rather*)
   _____

▶ **Practice 27. Modal auxiliary review.** (Chapter 7)
> The words in **bold** are modal auxiliaries. Read the passage, and then answer the question.

Doing Chores

Everyone in my family **has to** do chores around the house. A chore is a special job that one
person **must** perform. The chore **could** be to wash the dinner dishes, for example, or it **might** be
to sweep the porch. My parents give chores to my brother Joe and me, and we **have to** do these
chores every day.

Sometimes if one of us is busy and **can't** do a chore, the other one **may** take care of it. For
example, last Friday it was Joe's turn to wash the dishes after dinner. But he said he **couldn't** wash
them at that time because he had to hurry to school for a basketball game. Joe asked me, "**Will** you
do the dishes for me, please? I promise to do them for you tomorrow when it's your turn.
I**'ve got to** be on time for the game at school." I agreed to do Joe's chore and washed the dishes
after dinner.

But the next night, Joe "forgot" that we had traded days. When I reminded him to wash the
dishes, he said, "Who, me? It's not my turn."

In the future, we **should** put our agreements in writing. That **ought to** solve any problems if
anyone says, "It's not my turn."

What is the meaning of these modal auxiliaries from the passage? Circle the word or words closest
in meaning to the modal.

Modal Auxiliary		Meaning		
(1) Everyone **has to** do . . .	(must)	should	is able to	might
(2) . . . one person **must** perform . . .	has to	should	is able to	might
(3) The chore **could** be to wash . . .	must	should	is able to	might

(4) ... it **might** be to sweep ...	*must*	*should*	*is able to*	*could*
(5) ... we **have to** do these chores ...	*must*	*should*	*are able to*	*might*
(6) ... and **can't** do a chore ...	*must not*	*shouldn't*	*isn't able to*	*might not*
(7) ... the other one **may** ...	*must*	*should*	*is able to*	*might*
(8) But he said he **couldn't** ...	*must not*	*shouldn't*	*wasn't able to*	*may not*
(9) **Will** you do the dishes ...	*Must you*	*Should you*	*Are you able to*	*Would you*
(10) I've **got to** be on time ...	*must*	*should*	*am able to*	*may*
(11) ... we **should** put our ...	*must*	*ought to*	*are able to*	*may*
(12) That **ought to** solve ...	*must*	*should*	*is able to*	*may*

▶ **Practice 28. Editing.** (Chapter 7)
Correct the errors.

1. Before I left on my trip last month, I ~~must~~ *had to* get a passport.

2. Could you to bring us more coffee, please?

3. Ben can driving, but he prefers take the bus.

4. A few of our classmates can't to come to the school picnic.

5. May you take our picture, please?

6. Come in, come in! It's so cold outside. You must to be freezing!

7. Jim would rather has Fridays off in the summer than a long vacation.

8. I must reading several long books for my literature class.

9. Take your warm clothes with you. It will maybe snow.

10. It's such a gorgeous day. Why we don't go to a park or the beach?

► **Practice 29. Crossword puzzle.** (Chapter 7)
Complete the puzzle with modal auxiliaries. Use the clues to find the correct words.

Across

2. If you want to be a lawyer, you _____ to graduate from law school.

3. I _____ go with you. I don't know yet. If I finish my homework, I'll go with you.

5. _____ don't you join us for lunch today?

6. I'd _____ go fishing than go sailing.

7. You haven't eaten all day. You _____ be very hungry!

8. When I was a child, I _____ jump high into the air. Now I can't.

Down

1. Uh oh! You had _____ slow down! I see a police officer on his motorcycle over there.

3. _____ I come in? I'd like to talk to you.

4. I _____ study tonight, but I'm not going to. I'm going to watch a good movie on TV.

Index

Answer Key

CHAPTER 1: PRESENT TIME

PRACTICE 1, p. 1

1. is
2. name
3. is
4. am
5. am
6. meet
7. are
8. you
9. am
10. are
11. you
12. from
13. am
14. from
15. are
16. you
17. am
18. are
19. is
20. do
21. play OR meet
22. do
23. do
24. write
25. do
26. like
27. write
28. do
29. you
30. is
31. is
32. Is
33. is
34. is
35. is
36. is

PRACTICE 2, p. 2

1. am sitting
2. sit
3. do
4. am doing
5. am looking
6. am writing
7. is sitting
8. is working
9. works
10. is checking
11. checks
12. writes

PRACTICE 3, p. 3

Part I
1. speak
2. speak
3. speaks
4. speak
5. speaks

Part II
6. do not / don't speak
7. do not / don't speak
8. does not / doesn't speak
9. do not / don't speak
10. does not / doesn't speak

Part III
11. Do . . . speak
12. Do . . . speak
13. Does . . . speak
14. Do . . . speak
15. Does . . . speak

PRACTICE 4, p. 3

1. plays
2. conducts
3. collect
4. programs
5. trains
6. run
7. cooks
8. work
9. drives
10. write

PRACTICE 5, p. 4

1. doesn't point . . . points
2. doesn't come . . . comes
3. doesn't snow . . . snows
4. don't grow . . . grow
5. doesn't follow . . . follows
6. don't fly . . . fly
7. doesn't revolve . . . revolves
8. don't turn . . . turn

PRACTICE 6, p. 4

1. do
2. Ø
3. does
4. Ø
5. do
6. Ø
7. Ø . . . does
8. Ø
9. Ø
10. do
11. Do

PRACTICE 7, p. 5

Part I
1. am speaking
2. are speaking
3. is speaking
4. are speaking
5. is speaking

Part II
6. am not speaking
7. are not speaking
8. is not speaking
9. are not speaking
10. is not speaking

Part III
11. Are . . . speaking
12. Is . . . speaking
13. Are . . . speaking
14. Are . . . speaking
15. Is . . . speaking

PRACTICE 8, p. 5

1. is looking
2. is staring
3. are texting
4. is filing
5. are listening
6. is moving
7. is drawing
8. is sleeping
9. am trying
10. is speaking
11. is losing
12. is falling

PRACTICE 9, p. 6

Group 1
1. c
2. a
3. b

Group 2
1. c
2. b
3. a

Group 3
1. b
2. c
3. a

Group 4
1. b
2. a
3. c

PRACTICE 10, p. 6

1. Is he
2. Does he
3. Is he
4. Is he
5. Does he
6. Is he
7. Is he
8. Does he
9. Does he
10. Does he

PRACTICE 11, p. 7

1. Is she
2. Does she
3. Is she
4. Is she
5. Does she
6. Does she
7. Is she
8. Is she
9. Does she
10. Is she

PRACTICE 12, p. 7

1. b
2. a
3. a
4. c
5. b
6. b
7. a
8. a
9. a
10. c
11. c
12. c

PRACTICE 13, p. 8

1. usually . . . Ø
2. Ø . . . usually
3. always . . . Ø
4. Ø . . . always
5. usually . . . Ø
6. Ø . . . always
7. sometimes . . . Ø
8. never . . . Ø
9. Ø . . . never
10. Ø . . . usually . . . Ø
11. Ø . . . always . . . Ø
12. Ø . . . always

PRACTICE 14, p. 8

1. a. usually doesn't come
   b. doesn't ever come
   c. seldom comes
   d. sometimes doesn't come
   e. doesn't always come
   f. occasionally doesn't come
   g. never comes
   h. hardly ever comes
2. a. isn't usually
   b. is rarely
   c. isn't always
   d. isn't frequently
   e. is never
   f. isn't ever
   g. is seldom

PRACTICE 15, p. 9

1. always wakes
2. sometimes skips
3. frequently visits
4. is usually
5. seldom surfs
6. usually cleans
7. rarely does
8. is never

PRACTICE 16, p. 9

Part I
Verbs: are, form, have, call, are, occur, travel, cause, like, is coming
Frequency adverbs: Usually, often, never

Part II
1. T
2. F
3. F
4. F
5. T
6. F
7. F
8. T

PRACTICE 17, p. 10

1. Plural
2. Singular
3. Plural
4. Singular
5. Singular
6. Plural
7. Plural
8. Singular
9. Singular
10. Plural

PRACTICE 18, p. 10

1. eats
2. gets
3. teaches
4. works
5. does
6. studies
7. pays
8. has
9. buys
10. goes

PRACTICE 19, p. 11

Underlined verbs:
1. hop**s**
2. live (No change.)
3. carr**ies** . . . watch**es**
4. taste**s** . . . come**s**
5. are . . . contain (No change.)
6. bake**s** . . . cut**s** . . . put**s**
7. is . . . fix**es**
8. work**s** . . . **fries** . . . serve**s**
9. go . . . Fred go**es**

PRACTICE 20, p. 11

1. leaves
2. He walks
3. catches
4. he transfers
5. He arrives
6. He stays
7. he leaves
8. He attends
9. He
10. studies
11. tries
12. he goes
13. He has

PRACTICE 21, p. 12

1. a
2. a
3. b
4. b
5. a
6. a
7. b
8. a
9. b
10. a

PRACTICE 22, p. 12

1. is snowing
2. takes
3. drive
4. am watching
5. prefer
6. need
7. understand
8. belongs
9. is raining . . . is shining

PRACTICE 23, p. 13

1. usually doesn't take
2. needs
3. is enjoying
4. are
5. are eating
6. are drinking
7. (are) reading
8. is working
9. is feeding
10. are playing
11. knows
12. love
13. has
14. play
15. is smiling
16. relaxing
17. usually takes
18. is

PRACTICE 24, p. 13

1. Don **is** not working now.
2. Florida doesn't **have** mountains.
3. This train **is always** late.
4. Does Marta usually **go** to bed early?
5. Mr. Chin always come**s** to work on time.
6. Shh! The concert **is** starting now.
7. The refrigerator **does not (doesn't)** work.
8. **Does** Catherine **have** a car?
9. Pam and Bob are getting married. They **love** each other.
10. Anne **does** not understand this subject.
11. Jessica **sometimes asks** her parents for advice.
12. **Do** you do your laundry at the laundromat on the corner?
13. When the color blue mix**es** with the color yellow, the result is green.
14. Boris **fries** two eggs for breakfast every morning.
15. We are **studying** English.

PRACTICE 25, p. 14

1. A: Are
   B: I am OR I'm not
2. A: Do
   B: they do OR they don't
3. A: Do
   B: I do OR I don't
4. A: Does
   B: she does OR she doesn't
5. A: Are
   B: they are OR they aren't
6. A: Do
   B: they do OR they don't
7. A: Is
   B: he is OR he isn't
8. A: Are
   B: I am OR I'm not
9. A: Is
   B: it is OR it isn't
10. A: Do
    B: we do OR we don't

PRACTICE 26, p. 15

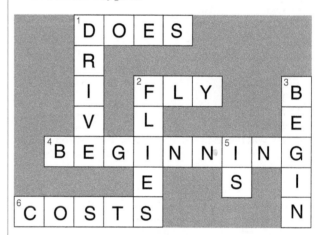

CHAPTER 2: PAST TIME

PRACTICE 1, p. 16

1. Did it start early? | It didn't start early.
2. Did Bob arrive late? | Bob didn't arrive late.
3. Was Hal here? | Hal wasn't here.
4. Did Dad plant roses? | Dad didn't plant roses.
5. Did Mom like the game? | Mom didn't like the game.
6. Did Kim cook dinner? | Kim didn't cook dinner.
7. Did Nat play tennis? | Nat didn't play tennis.
8. Were they late? | They weren't late.
9. Did Sam invite Ann? | Sam didn't invite Ann.
10. Did we do our work? | We didn't do our work.

PRACTICE 2, p. 16

Statement	Question	Negative
1.	Do you work	
2.	Did you work	You didn't work
3. She works	Does she work	
4.	Did she work	She didn't work
5. They work		They don't work
6.	Did they work	They didn't work
7. He works	Does he work	
8.	Did he work	He didn't work

PRACTICE 3, p. 17

1. A: Is
   B: isn't
2. A: Was
   B: was
3. A: Did
   B: did
4. A: Was
   B: wasn't
5. A: Was
   B: was
6. A: Was
   B: was
7. A: Was
   B: was
8. A: Did
   B: did
9. A: Is
   B: is
10. A: Did
    B: did

PRACTICE 4, p. 17

1. Did he study
2. Was he sick
3. Was she sad
4. Did they eat
5. Were they hungry
6. Did you go
7. Did she understand
8. Did he forget

PRACTICE 5, p. 18

1. Did
2. Was
3. Was
4. Were
5. Did
6. Did
7. Did
8. Were
9. Were
10. Are

PRACTICE 6, p. 18

1. A: Did you pass
   B: I did
2. A: Were you
   B: I wasn't
3. A: Did you practice
   B: I did
4. A: Was the test
   B: it wasn't
5. A: Did you make
   B: I didn't
6. A: Was the car
   B: it was
7. A: Did you put
   B: I did
8. A: Did you go
   B: I didn't

PRACTICE 7, p. 19

PRACTICE 8, p. 20

Double the consonant.	Drop the –e.	Just add -ing.
hitting	coming	learning
beginning	hoping	listening
cutting	smiling	raining
hopping	taking	staying
winning	writing	studying

PRACTICE 9, p. 20

1. waiting, wait
2. petting, pet
3. biting, bite
4. sitting, sit
5. writing, write
6. fighting, fight
7. waiting, wait
8. getting, get
9. starting, start
10. permitting, permit
11. lifting, lift
12. eating, eat
13. tasting, taste
14. cutting, cut
15. meeting, meet
16. visiting, visit

PRACTICE 10, p. 21

Part I

1. is beginning
2. are broadcasting
3. are running
4. are competing
5. are racing
6. is starting
7. are getting
8. are trying
9. are speeding
10. isn't raining
11. are worrying

Part II

1. cheered
2. shouted
3. enjoyed
4. raced
5. crossed
6. finished
7. occurred
8. crashed
9. needed
10. started
11. completed
12. happened

End of verb	Double the consonant?	Simple form	-ing	-ed
-e	No	live race	living racing	lived raced
Two Consonants	No	work start	working starting	worked started
Two Vowels + One Consonant	No	shout wait	shouting waiting	shouted waited
One Vowel + One Consonant	Yes	ONE-SYLLABLE VERBS pat shop	patting shopping	patted shopped
	No	TWO-SYLLABLE VERBS: STRESS ON FIRST SYLLABLE listen happen	listening happening	listened happened
	Yes	TWO-SYLLABLE VERBS: STRESS ON SECOND SYLLABLE occur refer	occurring referring	occurred referred
-y	No	play reply study	playing replying studying	played replied studied
-ie		die tie	dying tying	died tied

PRACTICE 11, p. 22
1. stopped
2. picked
3. arrive
4. crying
5. walk, walking
6. went
7. practiced
8. referred
9. made
10. hopped
11. hoped, hoping
12. put
13. eating
14. sing
15. listened, listening

PRACTICE 12, p. 23

Part I	Part III	Part V
bought	blew	hit
brought	drew	hurt
fought	flew	read
thought	grew	shut
taught	knew	cost
caught	threw	put
found		quit

Part II	Part IV	Part VI
swam	broke	paid
drank	wrote	said
sang	froze	
rang	rode	
	sold	
	stole	

PRACTICE 13, p. 23
1. was . . . flew . . . spent
2. came . . . took . . . put . . . lost
3. began . . . sang . . . became . . . knew . . . wore

PRACTICE 14, p. 24
1. walked . . . yesterday
2. talked . . . last
3. opened . . . yesterday
4. went . . . last
5. met . . . last
6. Yesterday . . . made . . . took
7. paid . . . last
8. Yesterday . . . fell
9. left . . . last

PRACTICE 15, p. 25
1. didn't fly . . . rode
2. aren't . . . are
3. wasn't . . . was (answers will vary)
4. didn't come . . . came
5. doesn't come . . . comes
6. didn't sleep . . . slept
7. isn't . . . is
8. didn't disappear . . . disappeared
9. don't make . . . make

PRACTICE 16, p. 26
1.		is	was
2.	think		thought
3.		are playing	played
4.	drink	am drinking	
5.	teaches		taught
6.	swims	is swimming	
7.		are sleeping	slept
8.	reads		read
9.	try	are trying	
10.		are eating	ate

PRACTICE 17, p. 26
1. were hiding
2. were singing
3. was watching
4. were talking
5. were reading . . . were sitting . . . looking

PRACTICE 18, p. 27
1. was playing . . . broke
2. scored . . . was playing
3. hurt . . . was playing
4. was hiking . . . found
5. saw . . . was hiking
6. picked up . . . was hiking
7. tripped . . . fell . . . was dancing
8. was dancing . . . met
9. was dancing . . . got

PRACTICE 19, p. 27
1. were walking
2. was washing . . . dropped . . . broke
3. saw . . . was eating . . . was talking . . . joined
4. was singing . . . did not hear
5. A: Did your lights go out
   B: was taking . . . found . . . ate . . . went . . . slept

PRACTICE 20, p. 28
1. d	5. g
2. c	6. h
3. b	7. f
4. a	8. e

PRACTICE 21, p. 28

                   1   2
1. The fire alarm sounded. Everyone left the building.
   When the fire alarm sounded, everyone left the building.

                   1   2
2. They left the building. They stood outside in the rain.
   After they left the building, they stood outside in the rain.

                   2   1
3. Everyone started to dance. The music began.
   As soon as the music began, everyone started to dance.

                   2   1
4. The music ended. They danced to all the songs.
   They danced to all the songs until the music ended.

5. The fans in the stadium applauded and cheered. (2)
   The soccer player scored a goal. (1)
   When the soccer player scored a goal, the fans in the stadium applauded and cheered.
6. Everyone left the stadium. (2) The game was over. (1)
   Everyone left the stadium as soon as the game was over.
7. I looked up her phone number. (1) I called her. (2)
   Before I called her, I looked up her phone number.
8. The phone rang 10 times. (1) I hung up. (2)
   I hung up after the phone rang 10 times.

PRACTICE 22, p. 29
1. used to hate school
2. used to be a secretary
3. used to play tennis
4. used to have fresh eggs
5. used to crawl under his bed . . . put his hands over his ears
6. used to go
7. used to wear
8. used to hate
9. used to eat

PRACTICE 23, p. 30
Part I
Underlined verbs: Do . . . orbit, do . . . orbit, orbit, is, is means, orbit.
Circled verbs: used to orbit, Did . . . disappear, did . . . disappear, changed, decided, reclassified, put, reclassified, orbited.

Part II
1. T
2. T
3. F
4. T
5. F
6. T
7. F

PRACTICE 24, p. 30
1. We **didn't visit** my cousins last weekend.
2. They **walked** to school yesterday.
3. I **understood** all the teacher's questions yesterday.
4. Matt and I were **talking** on the phone when the lights went out.
5. When Flora **heard** the news, she didn't **know** what to say.
6. David and Carol **went** to Italy last month.
7. I didn't **drive** a car when I **was** a teenager.
8. Carmen didn't **use(d)** to eat fish, but now she does.
9. Ms. Pepper didn't **die** in the accident.
10. **Did** you **see** that red light? You didn't **stop**!
11. I used to **live** in a big city when I was a child. Now I live in a small town.
12. Last night at about seven we **ate** a delicious pizza. Howard **made** the pizza in his new oven.
13. Sally **broke** her right foot last year. After that, she **hopped** on her left foot for three weeks.

PRACTICE 25, p. 31
1. was preparing
2. was playing
3. rang
4. was boiling
5. turned
6. answered
7. opened
8. saw
9. was holding
10. needed
11. screamed
12. fell
13. hurt
14. slammed
15. ran
16. heard
17. was waiting
18. opened
19. took
20. thanked
21. signed

PRACTICE 26, p. 31
1. a
2. b
3. b
4. a
5. c
6. c
7. b
8. b
9. c
10. b
11. a
12. a
13. c

PRACTICE 27, p. 32

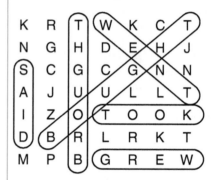

CHAPTER 3: FUTURE TIME

PRACTICE 1, p. 33
1. is going to be
4. will finish
5. will design
8. is going to live
10. 'll be

PRACTICE 2, p. 33
1. am going to leave
2. is going to leave
3. isn't going to leave
4. Are . . . going to leave
5. is going to be
6. are going to be
7. am not going to be
8. Is . . . going to be
9. is going to rain
10. isn't going to snow
11. isn't going to shine
12. Is . . . going to rain

1. is going to wake up
2. is going to catch
3. is going to jump
4. are going to fall

PRACTICE 4, p. 34

am going to	will
are going to	will
is going to	will
are going to	will
are going to	will
are not going to	will not / won't
is not going to	will not / won't
am not going to	will not / won't

PRACTICE 5, p. 35

The Smiths **will** celebrate their 50th wedding anniversary on December 1st of this year. Their children are planning a party for them at a local hotel. Their family and friends **will** join them for the celebration.

Mr. and Mrs. Smith have three children and five grandchildren. The Smiths know that two of their children **will** be at the party, but the third child, their youngest daughter, is far away in Africa, where she is doing medical research. They believe she **will** not come home for the party.

The Smiths don't know it, but their youngest daughter **will** be at the party. She is planning to surprise them. It **will** be a wonderful surprise for them! They **will** be very happy to see her. The whole family **will** enjoy being together for this special occasion.

PRACTICE 6, p. 35

1. Will Nick start
   Is Nick going to start
2. Will Mr. Jones give
   Is Mr. Jones going to give
3. Will Jacob quit
   Is Jacob going to quit
4. Will Mr. and Mrs. Kono adopt
   Are Mr. and Mrs. Kono going to adopt
5. Will the Johnsons move
   Are the Johnsons going to move
6. Will Dr. Johnson retire
   Is Dr. Johnson going to retire

PRACTICE 7, p. 36

1. Tomorrow will be
2. Will we have
3. we will have
4. Will the test be
5. will not be
6. Will I pass
7. You will pass
8. will not pass

PRACTICE 8, p. 36

1. a. arrives
   b. arrived
   c. is going to arrive
   d. will arrive
2. a. eats
   b. ate
   c. is going to eat
   d. will eat
3. a. doesn't arrive
   b. didn't arrive
   c. isn't going to arrive
   d. will not arrive
4. a. Do . . . eat
   b. Did . . . eat
   c. Are . . . going to eat
   d. Will . . . eat
5. a. don't eat
   b. didn't eat
   c. am not going to eat
   d. will not eat

PRACTICE 9, p. 37

1. 'll enjoy . . . 'll begin . . . 'll teach
2. 'll be . . . 'll call
3. 'll start . . . 'll ride . . . 'll drive

PRACTICE 10, p. 37

1. A: Will you / Are you going to help
   B: I will / am OR I won't / I'm not
2. A: Will Paul / Is Paul going to lend
   B: he will / is OR he won't / isn't
3. A: Will Jane / Is Jane going to graduate
   B: she will / is OR she won't / isn't
4. A: Will her parents / Are her parents going to be
   B: they will / are OR they won't / aren't
5. A: Will you / Are you going to answer
   B: I will / am OR I won't / I'm not
6. A: Will Jill / Is Jill going to text
   B: she will / is OR she won't / isn't

PRACTICE 11, p. 38

Part I
1. I'll probably go
2. she probably won't come
3. he'll probably go
4. he probably won't hand
5. they'll probably have

Part II
6. I'm probably going to watch
7. I'm probably not going to be
8. they probably aren't going to come
9. she probably isn't going to ride
10. it is probably going to be

PRACTICE 12, p. 39

	100% Certain	About 90% Certain	About 50% Certain
1.		✓	
2.			✓
3.			✓
4.		✓	
5.			✓
6.	✓		
7.	✓		
8.		✓	
9.			✓
10.		✓	
11.			✓
12.		✓	

PRACTICE 13, p. 39
1. are probably going to have
2. are probably not going to invite
3. may have . . . Maybe . . . will have
4. may rent
5. will probably decide
6. may not be . . . may be
7. will go
8. probably won't go

PRACTICE 14, p. 40
1. a
2. a
3. c
4. b
5. a
6. a
7. c
8. a
9. c
10. b
11. b

PRACTICE 15, p. 41
Part I
1. 'm going to work
2. 'm going to watch
3. 're going to move
4. 'm going to get

Part II
1. 'll answer
2. 'll ask
3. 'll clean
4. 'll pay

PRACTICE 16, p. 42
1. 'm going to
2. 'll
3. 'm going to
4. 'll
5. 'm going to . . . 'll

PRACTICE 17, p. 42
1. will
2. are going to
3. are going to
4. are going to
5. am going to
6. am going to
7. will

PRACTICE 18, p. 43
Underlined clauses:
1. Before Bill met Maggie
2. until he met Maggie.
3. When he met Maggie
4. after he met her
5. After they dated for a year
6. As soon as Bill gets a better job
7. before they buy a house
8. when they have enough money
9. After they get married
10. until they die

PRACTICE 19, p. 43
1. After I finish . . . I'm going to go
2. I'm not going to go . . . until I finish
3. Before Ann watches . . . she will finish
4. Jim is going to read . . . after he gets
5. When I call . . . I'll ask
6. Ms. Torres will stay . . . until she finishes
7. As soon as I get . . . I'm going to take

PRACTICE 20, p. 44
1. If it rains tomorrow,
2. If it is hot tomorrow,
3. if he has enough time
4. If I don't get a check tomorrow,
5. if I get a raise soon
6. If Gina doesn't study for her test,
7. if I have enough money
8. If I don't study tonight,

PRACTICE 21, p. 45
Sam and I are going to leave on a road trip tomorrow. We'll pack our suitcases and put everything in the car before we **go** to bed tonight. We'll leave tomorrow morning at dawn, as soon as the sun **comes** up. We'll drive for a couple of hours on the interstate highway while we **talk** and **listen** to our favorite music. When we **see** a nice rest area, we'll stop for coffee. After we **walk** around the rest area a little bit, we'll get back in the car and drive a little longer. We'll stay on that highway until we **come** to Highway 44. Then we'll turn off and drive on scenic country roads. If Sam **gets** tired, I'll drive. Then when I **drive,** he'll probably take a little nap. We'll keep going until it **gets** dark.

PRACTICE 22, p. 45
1. e
2. g
3. a
4. f
5. b
6. c
7. d

PRACTICE 23, p. 46
1. <u>When Sue has enough money,</u> she is going to buy an apartment. OR
   Sue is going to buy an apartment <u>when she has enough money</u>.
2. <u>Before my friends come over,</u> I'm going to clean up my apartment. OR
   I'm going to clean up my apartment <u>before my friends come over</u>.
3. <u>When the storm is over,</u> I'm going to do some errands. OR
   I'm going to do some errands <u>when the storm is over</u>.
4. <u>If you don't learn how to use a computer,</u> you will have trouble finding a job. OR
   You will have trouble finding a job <u>if you don't learn how to use a computer</u>.
5. <u>As soon as Joe finishes his report,</u> he is going to meet us at the coffee shop. OR
   Joe is going to meet us at the coffee shop <u>as soon as he finishes his report</u>.
6. <u>After Lesley washes and dries the dishes,</u> she will put them away. OR
   Lesley will put away the dishes <u>after she washes and dries them</u>.
7. <u>If they don't leave at seven,</u> they won't get to the theater on time. OR
   They won't get to the theater on time <u>if they don't leave at seven</u>.

PRACTICE 24, p. 46

1. will be
2. 'll get
3. 'll wash
4. brush
5. 'll put
7. 'll go
8. turn on
9. 'll walk
10. see
11. 'll watch
12. make
13. destroys
14. get
15. 'll pour
16. open
17. will come
18. 'll talk
19. 'll have
20. 'll make
21. say
22. 'll finish
23. 'll go
24. is
25. has
26. 'll work
27. will ring
28. 'll talk
29. 'll go
30. make
21. will be

PRACTICE 25, p. 48

1. I'm going to stay . . . I'm staying
2. They're going to travel . . . They're traveling
3. We're going to get . . . We're getting
4. He's going to start . . . He's starting
5. She's going to go . . . She's going
6. My neighbors are going to build . . . My neighbors are building

PRACTICE 26, p. 48

1. is traveling
2. is leaving
3. is speaking
4. are having
5. is . . . taking
6. are coming
7. am meeting
8. am graduating

PRACTICE 27, p. 49

1. b
2. a
3. a
4. b
5. b
6. a
7. b
8. a

PRACTICE 28, p. 49

1. a
2. a, b
3. a, b
4. a, b
5. a
6. a, b
7. a
8. a, b
9. a
10. a, b

PRACTICE 29, p. 50

1. A: does . . . begin / start
   B: begins / starts
2. opens
3. arrives / gets in
4. begins / starts
5. A: do . . . close
   B: closes
6. open . . . starts / begins . . . . arrive . . . ends / finishes
7. A: does . . . depart / leave
   B: leaves / departs
   B: does . . . arrive (get in)

PRACTICE 30, p. 51

1. d
2. f
3. a
4. h
5. b
6. c
7. g
8. e

PRACTICE 31, p. 51

1. study
2. set
3. doing
4. go
5. fell
6. is writing . . . is waiting
7. takes . . . buys
8. go . . . tell
9. am taking . . . forgetting
10. will discover . . . (will) apologize

PRACTICE 32, p. 52

1. My friends **will** join us after work.
2. Maybe the party **will end** / **is going to end** soon. OR The party **may end** soon.
3. On Friday, our school **will close** / **is going to close** early so teachers can go to a workshop.
4. It **will rain** / **is going to rain** tomorrow.
5. Our company is going to **sell** computer equipment to schools.
6. Give grandpa a hug. He's about to **leave.**
7. Mr. Scott is going to retire and **move** to a warmer climate.
8. If your soccer team **wins** the championship tomorrow, we'll have a big celebration for you.
9. I bought this cloth because **I'm going to** / **am going to** make some curtains for my bedroom.
10. I moving to London when I **finish** my education here.
11. Are you going **to go** to the meeting? OR Are you **going to** the meeting?
12. I opened the door and **walked** to the front of the room.
13. When **are** you going to move into your new apartment?
14. Maybe I **will** celebrate my 30th birthday with my friends at a restaurant. OR **I may** celebrate . . .

PRACTICE 33, p. 52

1. am working
2. need
3. go
4. am going to finish
5. write
6. stayed
7. was reading
8. heard
9. went
10. didn't see
11. went
12. found
13. made
14. is watching
15. always watches
16. is
17. is going to mow
18. am making
19. is cooking
20. were
21. used to make
22. got
23. are gong to go / are going
24. are
25. are going to see
26. bought
27. always buy
28. leave
29. usually stay
30. are
31. are not going to stay
32. tried
33. was
34. may stay
35. will stay
36. plays
37. skips
38. isn't doing
39. doesn't study
40. go
41. will / is going to flunk
42. saw
43. ran
44. caught
45. knocked
46. called
47. was waiting / waited
48. got
49. understood
50. put
51. took
52. ended
53. woke

(Crossword puzzle grid)

Across:
- ³RAINS
- ⁷ARRIVE
- ⁸MAYBE

Down:
- ¹PROBABLY
- ²WILL STARTS
- ⁴ARTS
- ⁵GOING
- ⁶BEGIN
- MAY

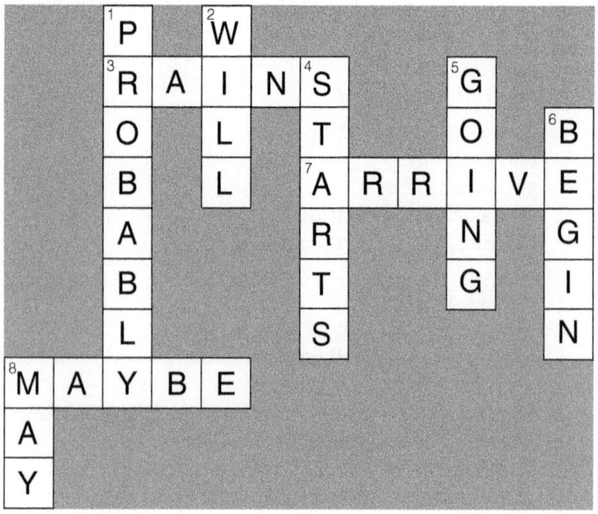

CHAPTER 4: PRESENT PERFECT AND PAST PERFECT

PRACTICE 1, p. 55

1. finished
2. stopped
3. put
4. known
5. been
6. wanted
7. said
8. had
9. gone
10. taken

PRACTICE 2, p. 55

Group I

Simple form	Simple past	Past participle
hurt	hurt	hurt
put	put	put
quit	quit	quit
upset	upset	upset
cut	cut	cut
shut	shut	shut
let	let	let
set	set	set

Group II

Simple form	Simple past	Past participle
ring	rang	rung
drink	drank	drunk
swim	swam	swum
sing	sang	sung
sink	sank	sunk

Group III

Simple Form	Simple Past	Past Participle
win	won	won
feed	fed	fed
weep	wept	wept
stand	stood	stood
keep	kept	kept
sit	sat	sat
stick	stuck	stuck
meet	met	met
have	had	had
find	found	found
buy	bought	bought
catch	caught	caught
fight	fought	fought
teach	taught	taught
pay	paid	paid
bring	brought	brought
think	thought	thought

PRACTICE 3, p. 56

1. has taught
2. has sold
3. has loved
4. have had
5. have known
6. have played
7. have gotten
8. have gone
9. have been
10. has been

PRACTICE 4, p. 57

1. since
2. for
3. since
4. for
5. for
6. since
7. since
8. since
9. since
10. for

PRACTICE 5, p. 57

1. I have been in this class **for** a month.
2. I have known my teacher **since** September.
3. Sam has wanted a dog **for** two years.
4. Sara has needed a new car **since** last year / **for** a year.
5. Our professor has been sick **for** a week / **since** last week.
6. My parents have lived in Canada **since** December.
7. I have known Mrs. Brown **since** 1999.
8. Tom has worked at a fast-food restaurant **for** three weeks.

PRACTICE 6, p. 57

1. A: Have you ever eaten
   B: have . . . have eaten OR haven't . . . have never eaten
2. A: Have you ever talked
   B: have . . . have talked OR haven't . . . have never talked
3. A: Has Erica ever rented
   B: has . . . has rented OR hasn't . . . has never rented
4. A: Have you ever seen
   B: have . . . have seen OR haven't . . . have never seen
5. A: Has Joe ever caught
   B: has . . . has caught OR hasn't . . . has never caught
6. A: Have you ever had
   B: have . . . have had OR haven't . . . have never had
7. A: Have I ever met
   B: have . . . have met OR haven't . . . have never met
8. A: Have the boys ever been
   B: have . . . have been OR haven't . . . have never been

1. have you been
2. have you made
3. Have you always enjoyed
4. have
5. have you traveled
6. have been
7. have never wanted
8. Have you ever thought
9. haven't
10. haven't met

PRACTICE 8, p. 59
1.	b	5.	b
2.	a	6.	a, b
3.	a, b	7.	a
4.	a	8.	a

PRACTICE 9, p. 60
1. has not started school yet
2. has already learned the alphabet
3. has already corrected our tests
4. has not returned the tests yet
5. has not cooked dinner yet
6. has already cooked dinner

PRACTICE 10, p. 60
1. haven't met all my neighbors yet
2. has traveled
3. has already changed
4. has already given
5. hasn't invited
6. have just retired
7. haven't seen
8. haven't picked
9. has lived
10. have already spent

PRACTICE 11, p. 61
1.	has . . . put	5.	have met
2.	has drunk	6.	have . . . found
3.	has . . . begun	7.	have . . . paid
4.	has won	8.	have bought

PRACTICE 12, p. 62
1.	C	8.	F
2.	F	9.	C
3.	F	10.	C
4.	F	11.	F
5.	C	12.	F
6.	F	13.	C
7.	F	14.	C

PRACTICE 13, p. 62
1. a, c, e, g, h
2. c, e, f, i

PRACTICE 14, p. 63
1.	c, i	4.	j, d
2.	k, e	5.	l, f
3.	a, g	6.	b, h

PRACTICE 15, p. 63
(1) started, was, had, has become, has been
(2) has led, has made, took, went, have gone, hasn't ended

PRACTICE 16, p. 64
1. have been waiting . . . twenty minutes
2. has been watching . . . two hours
3. has been working . . . 7:00 this morning
4. has been driving . . . six hours
5. has been writing . . . three years
6. have been arguing . . . Jim brought home a stray cat
7. has been raining . . . two days
8. has been losing . . . she began her diet OR her birthday

PRACTICE 17, p. 64
1.	F	3.	T	5.	T
2.	F	4.	F	6.	F

PRACTICE 18, p. 64
1.	b	5.	a
2.	b	6.	a
3.	a	7.	b
4.	b	8.	a

PRACTICE 19, p. 65
1. has been getting
2. have known
3. have been studying
4. have collected / have been collecting
5. have risen
6. has become

PRACTICE 20, p. 66
1. need
2. is
3. Have you ever worked
4. have worked / 've worked
5. had
6. did you work
7. have worked / 've worked
8. have never had
9. did you like
10. did not like / didn't like
11. was
12. are you working
13. do not have / don't have
14. have not had / haven't had
15. quit
16. Are you looking
17. am going to go / 'm going
18. is looking
19. will do / 'll do
20. have never looked / 've never looked
21. will be / is
22. do not know / don't know
23. will find / 'll find
24. go

PRACTICE 21, p. 67
1. <u>2</u> Larry called Jane.
   <u>1</u> Jane went out.
2. <u>2</u> I opened the door.
   <u>1</u> Someone knocked on the door.

3. 1 Her boyfriend called.
   2 My sister was happy.
4. 2 Our dog stood at the front door.
   1 He saw me putting on my coat.
5. 2 Ken laughed at my joke.
   1 Ken heard the joke many times.
6. 2 Don opened his car door with a wire hanger.
   1 Don lost his keys.

PRACTICE 22, p. 67
Underlined words:
(1) had always watched
(2) had always read
(3) had never let . . . had always listened
(4) had always left
(5) 'd never put
(6) had never shared

1. had always watched
2. had always read
3. had never let
4. had always left
5. had never put
6. had never shared

PRACTICE 23, p. 68
1. c   4. d
2. f   5. b
3. e   6. a

PRACTICE 24, p. 68
1. A: Did you enjoy
   B: enjoyed
2. A: Did you see
   B: was . . . hadn't seen
3. A: haven't seen
   B: is . . . haven't seen
4. A: Did you get
   B: got . . . had already begun
5. had already gone
6. have painted
7. have you painted
8. A: were painting . . . walked
   B: have been painting

PRACTICE 25, p. 69
1. Where were you? I **have been** waiting for you for an hour.
2. Anna **has** been a soccer fan **for** a long time.
3. Since I **was** a child, I have liked to solve puzzles.
4. Have you ever **wanted** to travel around the world?
5. The family **has been** at the hospital since they **heard** about the accident.
6. My sister is only 30 years old, but her hair has **begun** to turn gray.
7. Jake has been working as a volunteer at the children's hospital **for** several years.
8. Steve has worn his black suit only once since he **bought** it.
9. My cousin **has been** studying for medical school exams since last month.
10. I don't know the results of my medical tests **yet.** I'll find out soon.
11. The phone **had** already stopped ringing when Michelle entered her apartment.

PRACTICE 26, p. 70

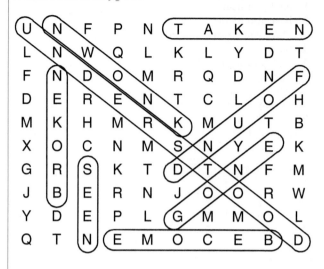

CHAPTER 5: ASKING QUESTIONS

PRACTICE 1, p. 71
1. c   4. c, a
2. b   5. b
3. a   6. b

PRACTICE 2, p. 72
1. Do you like coffee?
2. Does Tom like coffee?
3. Is Pietro watching TV?
4. Are you having lunch with Raja?
5. Did Rafael walk to school?
6. Was Clarita taking a nap?
7. Will Ted come to the meeting?
8. Is Ingrid a good artist?
9. Were you at the wedding?

PRACTICE 3, p. 73
1. A: Is   5: A: Have
   B: is   B: haven't
2. A: Is   6. A: Did
   B: isn't   B: didn't
3. A: Does   7. A: Are
   B: does   B: am
4. A: Do   8. A: Will
   B: do   B: will

PRACTICE 4, p. 73
1. A: Do   6. A: Does
   B: don't   B: does
2. A: Are   7. A: Is
   B: aren't   B: is
3. A: Is   8. A: Does
   B: isn't   B: doesn't
4. A: Do   9. A: Will
   B: do   B: won't
5. A: Do
   B: don't

1. A: Does Jane
   B: she does
2. A: Does George
   B: he doesn't
3. A: Did Jane and Anna
   B: they did
4. A: Did Jane
   B: she didn't
5. A: Did George
   B: he did
6. A: Did Jane and Anna
   B: they didn't
7. A: Did George and John
   B: they did
8. A: Will Jane
   B: she will
9. A: Will George and Anna
   B: they will
10. A: Will John
    B: he won't

PRACTICE 6, p. 75
1. does Phil work
2. does Phil work
3. is Marta making
4. did she say
5. did Jean and Don visit
6. did they visit her

PRACTICE 7, p. 75
1. Does
2. Where
3. Is
4. When
5. Will
6. When
7. Are
8. Where
9. Is
10. Where
11. Did
12. When

PRACTICE 8, p. 76

Question word	Helping verb	Subject	Main verb	Rest of sentence
1. Ø	Did	you	hear	the news yesterday?
2. When	did	you	hear	the news?
3. Ø	Is	Eric	traveling	in South America?
4. Where	is	Eric	traveling?	
5. Ø	Will	the class	end	in December?
6. When	will	the class	end?	
7. Ø	Did	the teacher	help	a student?
8. Who(m)	did	the teacher	help?	
9. Ø	Will	the chef	cook	his special chicken dinner tonight?
10. What	will	the chef	cook	tonight?

PRACTICE 9, p. 77
1. Where did apple trees originate (b)
2. Where do apple trees grow (b)
3. Do they grow (a)
4. Do the trees produce apples (a)
5. When do they produce (b)
6. What do you find (b)
7. Will some of the seeds become (a)

PRACTICE 10, p. 78
1. d   4. b
2. e   5. f
3. c   6. a

PRACTICE 11, p. 78
1. a. you are going downtown
   b. are you going downtown
2. a. did Paul leave early for
   b. Paul left early
3. a. are your clothes on the floor
   b. are your clothes on the floor for
4. a. Mira needs money
   b. does Mira need money

PRACTICE 12, p. 78
1. Why are you waiting
2. When does Rachel start
3. Why did you miss
4. When are you leaving
5. When do you expect
6. Where did you eat lunch
7. What time did you eat
8. Why do you eat lunch
9. Where does the bullet train go
10. When will they build a bullet train
11. Where did you study
12. Why did you study

PRACTICE 13, p. 79
1. S   Who is talking
2. O   Who(m) do we hear
3. O   Who(m) do you know . . .
4. S   Who was on TV . . .
5. S   What is happening . . .
6. O   What does Jason know
7. O   Who(m) did Gilda call
8. S   Who answered the phone
9. O   What did you say
10. S   What is important

PRACTICE 14, p. 80

Part I
1. What
2. Who
3. Who
4. What
5. Who
6. What

Part II
1. Who(m)
2. Who
3. What
4. What
5. What
6. What

PRACTICE 15, p. 80
1. Who knows Julio?
2. Who(m) does Julio know?
3. Who will help us?
4. Who(m) will you ask?
5. Who(m) is Eric talking to?
6. Who is knocking on the door?
7. What surprised them?
8. What did Jack say?
9. What did Sue talk about?
10. Who(m) did Rosa talk about?

PRACTICE 16, p. 81
1. Who taught . . .
2. What did Robert see
3. Who got . . .
4. What are you making
5. Who(m) does that cell phone belong . . .
6. What is . . .

PRACTICE 17, p. 81

Answers will vary.
1. What does *abroad* mean
   It means in a foreign country
2. What does *underneath* mean
   It means directly under another object
3. What does *mild* mean
   It means fairly warm, not cold (when you are talking about the weather)
4. What does *cool* mean
   It means very attractive, fashionable, and interesting (when you are talking about a person)
5. What does *industrious* mean
   It means hard-working

PRACTICE 18, p. 82
1. What is Alex doing . . .
2. What did you do . . .
3. What do astronauts do . . .
4. What are you going to do . . .
5. What did Sara do . . .
6. What is Emily going to do . . .
7. What do you want to do . . .
8. What does Nick do . . .

PRACTICE 19, p. 82
1. Which
2. What
3. What
4. Which . . . which
5. What
6. which
7. What
8. What . . . which

PRACTICE 20, p. 83
1. What kind of music . . .
2. What kind of clothes . . .
3. What kind of Italian food . . .
4. What kind of books . . .
5. What kind of car . . .
6. What kind of government . . .
7. What kind of job . . .
8. What kind of person . . .

PRACTICE 21, p. 83
1. Who
2. Whose
3. Whose
4. Who
5. Who
6. Who
7. Whose

PRACTICE 22, p. 84
1. Whose house is that?
2. Who's living in that house?
3. Whose umbrella did you borrow?
4. Whose book did you use?
5. Whose book is on the table?
6. Who's on the phone?
7. Who's that?
8. Whose is that?

PRACTICE 23, p. 84
1. hot . . . hot
2. soon
3. expensive
4. busy . . . busy
5. serious . . . serious
6. safe
7. fresh . . . fresh
8. well . . . well

PRACTICE 24, p. 85
1. How often
2. How many times
3. How many times
4. How often
5. How often
6. How many times

PRACTICE 25, p. 85
1. How far is it
   How many miles is it
   How long does it take
2. How high is Mount Everest
   How many meters is Mount Everest
   How long did it take . . .
   How many days did it take . . .
3. How long is . . .
   How many miles is . . .
   How many days does it take . . .

PRACTICE 26, p. 86
1. far
2. long
3. often
4. far
5. far
6. long
7. high
8. long
9. often
10. far
11. long
12. often

PRACTICE 27, p. 87
1. How do you spell your name
2. How do you like . . .
3. How do you say . . .
4. How do you pronounce . . .
5. How do you feel . . .

PRACTICE 28, p. 87
1. a
2. b
3. c
4. a
5. b
6. c

PRACTICE 29, p. 88
1. will the clothes be dry
2. did you do
3. book did you download
4. long did it take
5. bread do you like
6. are you calling me
7. are you meeting
8. is taking you
9. you are leaving

PRACTICE 30, p. 89
1. What is Jack doing . . .
2. Who(m) is he playing . . .
3. What is Anna doing
4. What is she throwing . . .
5. What are Anna and Jack holding
6. What is . . .
7. Where are they
8. How long have they been playing
9. Who is winning . . .
10. Who won . . .

PRACTICE 31, p. 90
1. a. don't
   b. doesn't
   c. don't
   d. doesn't
   e. aren't
   f. doesn't
   g. do
   h. is
   i. am
2. a. didn't
   b. didn't
   c. wasn't
   d. did
   e. didn't
3. a. aren't
   b. is
   c. isn't
   d. wasn't
   e. wasn't
   f. were
4. a. hasn't
   b. haven't
   c. have
   d. hasn't
   e. has
   f. have

PRACTICE 32, p. 90
1. A: haven't you
   B: Yes, I have
2. A: has he
   B: No, he hasn't
3. A: didn't you
   B: Yes, I did
4. A: don't you
   B: Yes, I do
5. a. haven't they
   b. Yes, they have
6. a. hasn't she
   b. Yes, she has
7. a. is it
   b. No, it isn't
8. A: doesn't he
   B: Yes, he does

9. A: is it
   B: No, it isn't
10. A: is it
    B: No, it isn't
11. A: weren't they
    B: Yes, they were
12. A: will she
    B: No, she won't

PRACTICE 33, p. 91
1. **Who** saw the car accident?
2. How about **asking** Julie and Tim to come for dinner Friday night?
3. What time **does class begin** today?
4. Where **do** people go to get a driver's license in this city?
5. How long **does it take** to get to the beach from here?
6. She is working late tonight, **isn't** she?
7. **Whose** glasses are those?
8. **How tall is** your father?
9. Who **did you talk** / **have you talked** to about registration for next term?
10. How come **you are** here so early today?

PRACTICE 34, p. 92
1. When are you going to buy
2. How are you going to pay
3. How long have you had
4. How often do you ride
5. How do you usually get
6. Did you ride
7. Who gave
8. Did you ride
9. How far did you ride
10. Does your bike have
11. What kind of bike do you have
12. When did Jason get
13. Who broke
14. How did he break it
15. Did Billy get hurt
16. Did the bike have a lot of damage
17. Which wheel fell off
18. Has Jason fixed the bike yet

PRACTICE 35, p. 93

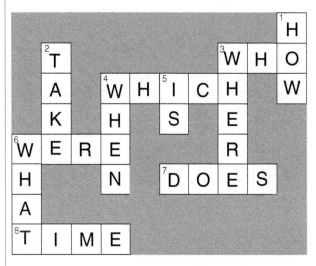

CHAPTER 6: NOUNS AND PRONOUNS

PRACTICE 1, p. 94

A (shark) is a (fish). <u>Sharks</u> live in <u>oceans</u> all over the (world). Some <u>types</u> are very large. The largest (shark) is the (size) of a (bus). It has 3,000 <u>teeth</u>, in five <u>rows</u> in its (mouth). When one (tooth) falls out, a new (tooth) grows in quickly. Many <u>sharks</u> are dangerous, and <u>people</u> try to avoid them.

PRACTICE 2, p. 94

Living things that breathe	Furniture	Places on a map	Fruits and Vegetables
children	beds	cities	apples
foxes	lamps	countries	cherries
men	shelves	lakes	carrots
mice	tables	oceans	peaches
cats		rivers	tomatoes
tigers			

PRACTICE 3, p. 95

1. houses
2. door
3. boxes
4. shelf
5. copies
6. families
7. woman
8. children
9. fish
10. fly
11. dishes
12. glasses
13. dollar
14. euros
15. roof
16. lives
17. radios

PRACTICE 4, p. 95

Underlined nouns:
1. Airplane**s** . . . wing**s**
2. bab**ies** . . . **teeth**
3. Child**ren** . . . swing**s**
4. No change.
5. potato**es**, bean**s**, pea**s**, . . . tomato**es**
6. No change.
7. animal**s** . . . zoo**s**
8. Humans . . . **feet**
9. No change.
10. Government**s** . . . tax**es**

PRACTICE 5, p. 96

        S   V   O
1. Caroline dropped a dish.
          S   V
2. The dish fell.
          S   V   O
3. The noise woke her baby.
          S   V
4. The baby cried.
         S   V   O
5. Caroline rocked her baby.
          S   V
6. The phone rang.
          S   V
7. A man came to the door.
          S   V
8. The dog barked loudly
          S   V   O
9. Caroline answered the door.

PRACTICE 6, p. 96

	subject	verb	object of verb
1.	Children	play	Ø
2.	Children	like	ice cream
3.	A package	arrived	Ø
4.	The mail carrier	delivered	the package
5.	My mother	sent	the package
6.	The passengers	boarded	the airplane
7.	The plane	left	the gate
8.	The plane	left	Ø

PRACTICE 7, p. 97

1. N
2. V
3. N
4. V
5. V
6. N
7. N
8. V
9. N
10. V
11. V
12. N

PRACTICE 8, p. 97

1. in
2. on
3. on
4. beside
5. above
6. below
7. behind
8. at
9. into
10. out

PRACTICE 9, p. 98

1. f
2. e
3. d
4. c
5. b
6. a

PRACTICE 10, p. 98

1. in / into . . . on
2. in . . . of
3. near . . . to
4. above . . . below
5. of
6. through . . . on
7. from

PRACTICE 11, p. 99

Part I
Circled words:
(1) in, in, over, through, on, under, into
(2) after, around, across, on, against, near
(3) behind, beneath

Underlined words:
(1) Jamaica, sky, beaches, trees, roof, door, house
(2) storm, neighborhood, street, ground, house, house
(3) clouds, sun

Part II
1. Dark clouds appeared in the sky.
2. The water came in under the door.
3. After the storm, the people walked around the neighborhood.
4. The tree had fallen on the ground/ across the street.
5. The sun had been behind the clouds.
6. The neighbors felt happy and grateful when they were standing beneath the hot Jamaican sun.

PRACTICE 12, p. 100
1. in
2. in
3. on
4. on
5. at
6. at
7. in
8. on
9. at
10. at
11. in
12. on
13. in
14. in
15. on

PRACTICE 13, p. 100
1. at . . . in . . . in . . . on . . . on
2. on . . . At . . . at . . . in . . . In

PRACTICE 14, p. 100
1. to the airport tomorrow morning
2. a new job last month
3. skis in the mountains in January
4. has breakfast at the coffee shop in the morning
5. jogged in the park last Sunday
6. bought a house in the suburbs last year

PRACTICE 15, p. 101
1. 1 the driver.
   2 at a busy intersection.
   3 at midnight.
2. 2 on the lake.
   3 last summer.
   1 a sailboat.
3. 2 in the river.
   1 several fish.
   3 last weekend.
4. 3 at noon.
   1 our lunch.
   2 in the park.
5. 1 a magazine.
   2 at the corner newsstand.
   3 after work yesterday.

PRACTICE 16, p. 101
1. are
2. are
3. is
4. is
5. are
6. is
7. are
8. is
9. are
10. are
11. is

PRACTICE 17, p. 101
1. make
2. need
3. Do
4. are
5. are
6. comes
7. is
8. pay
9. are
10. needs
11. go
12. work
13. are

PRACTICE 18, p. 102
1. loud → voice
2. sweet → sugar
3. easy → test
4. free → air
5. delicious → food . . . Mexican → restaurant
6. sick → child
7. sick → child . . . warm → bed . . . hot → tea

PRACTICE 19, p. 102
1. old
2. old
3. bad
4. easy
5. hard
6. narrow
7. clean
8. empty
9. safe
10. light
11. light
12. public
13. right
14. right
15. long

PRACTICE 20, p. 103
1. page numbers
2. paper money
3. apartment buildings
4. rose gardens
5. key chains
6. city governments
7. brick walls
8. egg cartons
9. mountain views
10. traffic lights
11. apple pies
12. steel bridges

PRACTICE 21, p. 103
1. b
2. c
3. a
4. b
5. b
6. a

PRACTICE 22, p. 104
1. T
2. T
3. T
4. T
5. F

PRACTICE 23, p. 104
1. The **mountains** in Chile are beautiful.
2. **Cats** hunt **mice**
3. **Mosquitos** are small **insects**.
4. Everyone has **eyelashes**.
5. Do you listen to any podcasts when you take plane **trips**?
6. **Forests** sometimes have **fires**. Forest **fires** endanger wild **animals**.

7. Sharp kitchen **knives** can be dangerous.
8. I couldn't get **concert** tickets for Friday. The **tickets** were all sold out.
9. There are approximately 250,000 different **kinds** of **flowers** in the world.
10. I applied to several foreign **universities** because I want to study in a different **country**.
11. Ted lives with three other university **students**.
12. In the past one hundred **years**, our daily **lives** have changed in many **ways**. We no longer need to use oil **lamps** or **candles** in our **houses**, raise our own **chickens**, or build daily **fires** for cooking.

PRACTICE 24, p. 105
1. a. her → Dr. Gupta
   b. She → Dr. Gupta
   c. them → students
   d. They → students
   e. they → classes
2. a. him → Dr. Reynolds
   b. He → Dr. Reynolds
   c. them → patients
   d. he → Dr. Reynolds
   e. him → Dr. Reynolds
3. a. It → my hometown
   b. I → Beth
   c. They → the people
   d. me → Beth
   e. They → the people
   f. you → you (the reader of this passage)
   g. they → the people
   h. you → you (the reader of this passage)

PRACTICE 25, p. 106
1. O
2. S
3. S
4. O
5. S
6. O
7. S
8. S
9. O
10. S
11. O
12. O
13. S
14. O

PRACTICE 26, p. 106
1. me, them, us, you, her, him
2. He, You, I, She, They, We
3. him and me, you and me, her and me, them and us
4. He and I, She and I, You and I

PRACTICE 27, p. 107
1. me
2. me
3. I
4. She
5. she . . . her
6. he . . . him
7. us . . . us
8. them . . . They

PRACTICE 28, p. 107
1. a
2. b
3. b
4. a
5. a
6. b
7. a
8. b
9. a
10. a

PRACTICE 29, p. 108
1. friend's
2. friends'
3. parents'
4. mother's
5. Carl's
6. Carl's
7. baby's
8. baby's
9. babies'
10. Ann's
11. Bob's
12. James's / James'

PRACTICE 30, p. 108
1. I met **Dan's** sister yesterday.
2. No change.
3. I know **Jack's** roommates.
4. No change.
5. I have one roommate. My **roommate's** desk is always messy.
6. You have two roommates. Your **roommates'** desks are always neat.
7. No change.
8. Jo Ann is **Betty's** sister. My **sister's** name is Sonya.
9. My name is Richard. I have two sisters. My **sisters'** names are Jo Ann and Betty.
10. I read a book about the changes in **women's** roles and **men's** roles in modern society.

PRACTICE 31, p. 108
1. your . . . yours
2. her, hers
3. his, his
4. your, yours
5. their, our, theirs, ours

PRACTICE 32, p. 109
1. her
2. hers
3. Our
4. theirs
5. your
6. mine . . . my . . . yours
7. their . . . theirs
8. mine . . . yours

PRACTICE 33, p. 109
1. myself
2. ourselves
3. himself
4. herself
5. themselves
6. yourself
7. yourselves
8. itself

PRACTICE 34, p. 110
1. cut myself
2. be proud of yourself
3. talks to himself
4. taught myself
5. blamed herself
6. help yourselves
7. takes care of himself
8. enjoyed themselves
9. worked for himself
10. introduce themselves

PRACTICE 35, p. 110
1. me . . . him
2. yourselves
3. itself
4. its . . . its
5. hers
6. him
7. yourself . . . your
8. our . . . our
9. ours
10. themselves
11. itself
12. himself

PRACTICE 36, p. 111

(1)
1. his
2. He
3. himself
4. he
5. him

(2)
1. Her
2. her
3. She
4. Our
5. We
6. It
7. her
8. mine
9. hers
10. I

(3)
1. He
2. his
3. his
4. Her
5. They
6. themselves
7. them
8. my
9. theirs
10. their

PRACTICE 37, p. 112

1. one . . . another . . . another . . . the other
2. one . . . another . . . the other
3. one . . . another . . . another . . . another . . . the other
4. one . . . the other
5. one . . . another . . . another . . . another . . . another . . . the other

PRACTICE 38, p. 112

1. The other
2. Another
3. The other
4. a. Another
   b. the other
5. a. another
   b. another
   c. another
   d. another
   e. another

PRACTICE 39, p. 113

1. The others
2. The others
3. Others
4. others
5. other
6. Others
7. Other
8. The others
9. The other

PRACTICE 40, p. 113

1. a
2. a
3. c
4. d
5. b
6. b
7. a
8. d
9. b

PRACTICE 41, p. 114

1. are
2. potatoes
3. by myself
4. on . . . at
5. vacation
6. us
7. its
8. our . . . yours
9. himself
10. the others

PRACTICE 42, p. 114

1. Look at those **beautiful** mountains!
2. The children played **a game** on Saturday afternoon at the park.
3. There are two **horses**, several **sheep**, and a cow in the **farmer's** field.
4. The owner of the store is busy **at** the moment.
5. The teacher met **her** students at the park after school.
6. Everyone **wants** peace in the world.
7. I grew up in a **very large city**.
8. This apple tastes sour. There are more, so let's try **another** one.
9. Some **trees** lose their **leaves** in the winter.
10. I am going to wear my **blue shirt** to the party.
11. People may hurt **themselves** if they use this machine.
12. Our neighbors invited my friend and **me** to visit **them**.
13. My **husband's** boss works for twelve **hours** every **day**.
14. The students couldn't find **their** books.
15. I always read **magazine** articles while I'm in the waiting room at my **dentist's** office.

PRACTICE 43, p. 115

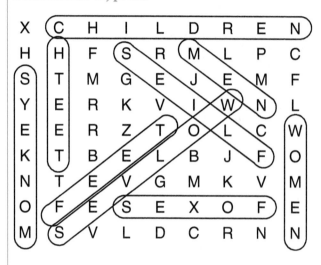

CHAPTER 7: MODAL AUXILIARIES

PRACTICE 1, p. 116

1. Ø
2. to
3. Ø
4. Ø
5. to
6. Ø
7. to
8. Ø
9. Ø . . . Ø
10. Ø . . . to
11. Ø . . . Ø

PRACTICE 2, p. 116

1. zebra
2. cat
3. Elephants
4. Monkeys
5. camels
6. cow
7. horse
8. donkey
9. squirrel
10. ants

PRACTICE 3, p. 117

1. possibility
2. possibility
3. permission
4. possibility
5. possibility
6. permission
7. possibility
8. permission
9. possibility
10. permission

PRACTICE 4, p. 117

1. I might take a nap.
2. Maybe she is sick.
3. Maybe there will be time later.
4. Our team may win.
5. You might be right.
6. We may hear soon.
7. It may rain.
8. It might snow.
9. Maybe she will come tomorrow.
10. Maybe she is at home right now.

PRACTICE 5, p. 118

1. b
2. c
3. c
4. a
5. b
6. a

PRACTICE 6, p. 118

1. b
2. b
3. a
4. a
5. b
6. a
7. b
8. a

PRACTICE 7, p. 119

1. e
2. d
3. f
4. b
5. c
6. a

PRACTICE 8, p. 119

1. May
2. Would
3. May
4. Would
5. will / could
6. Could
7. Will / Could

PRACTICE 9, p. 120

1. Could, Can, Would
2. Could, May, Can
3. Would, Could, Will
4. Can, May, Could
5. Will, Can, Could

PRACTICE 10, p. 120

1. shouldn't drive a long distance
2. should quit
3. should drive the speed limit
4. shouldn't give too much homework
5. should attend all classes
6. shouldn't be cruel to animals
7. should always be on time for an appointment
8. shouldn't throw trash out of your car window

PRACTICE 11, p. 121

1. j . . . i
2. e . . . f
3. b . . . g
4. h . . . d
5. a . . . c

PRACTICE 12, p. 122

1. a
2. c
3. b
4. a
5. b
6. c
7. a
8. c
9. b
10. c

PRACTICE 13, p. 122

1. have
2. must
3. has
4. had
5. have
6. have
7. had
8. have

PRACTICE 14, p. 123

1. had to
2. had to
3. have to
4. had to
5. have to
6. had to
7. have got to . . . have to
8. must

PRACTICE 15, p. 123

1. had to study
2. had to turn off
3. Did . . . have to work
4. had to see
5. had to be
6. had to close

PRACTICE 16, p. 124

1. You didn't stop at the red light. You have to stop at red lights.
2. You've got to be more responsible.
3. You have to send them back and get the right ones.
4. Okay. Everyone must fill out an application. Here it is.
5. No. He just has to stay in bed for a couple of days and drink plenty of water.

PRACTICE 17, p. 124

1. must
2. don't have to
3. must not
4. don't have to
5. don't have to
6. must not
7. must not
8. don't have to
9. must not
10. don't have to
11. must not

PRACTICE 18, p. 125

People have to / must
eat and drink in order to live
pay taxes
stop when they see a police car's lights behind them

People must not
fall asleep while driving
drive without a license
take other people's belongings

People don't have to
cook every meal themselves
say "sir" or "madam" to others
stay in their homes in the evening

PRACTICE 19, p. 126

1. c
2. d
3. e
4. a
5. b

PRACTICE 20, p. 126

1. 2
2. 1
3. 2
4. 1
5. 2
6. 2
7. 2
8. 1

PRACTICE 21, p. 126

1. will
2. can't
3. wouldn't
4. wouldn't
5. can
6. do
7. should
8. won't
9. could
10. shouldn't
11. doesn't
12. shouldn't

PRACTICE 22, p. 127

1. Wait
2. Don't wait
3. Read
4. Don't put
5. Come in . . . have

PRACTICE 23, p. 127

1. 1, 3, 2
2. 2, 1, 4, 3
3. 4, 2, 1, 3

PRACTICE 24, p. 128

Part I	*Part II*	*Part III*
1. fly	5. go	8. have
2. sail	6. shop	9. do
3. walk	7. see	10. plan
4. listen		11. tell

PRACTICE 25, p. 129

1. prefer
2. like
3. would rather
4. would rather
5. A: prefer
   B: likes . . . would rather
6. B: prefer
   A: like

PRACTICE 26, p. 129

1. Alex prefers swimming to jogging.
2. My son would rather eat fish than beef.
3. Kim prefers salad to dessert
4. In general, Nicole likes coffee better than tea.
5. Bill would rather teach history than work as a business executive.
6. When considering a pet, Sam likes dogs better than cats.
7. On a long trip, Susie prefers driving to riding in the back seat.
8. I would rather study in a noisy room than study in a quiet room.
9. Alex would rather play soccer than baseball.

PRACTICE 27, p. 130

1. must
2. has to
3. might
4. could
5. must
6. isn't able to
7. might
8. wasn't able to
9. Would you
10. must
11. ought to
12. should

PRACTICE 28, p. 131

1. Before I left on my trip last month, I **had to** get a passport.
2. Could **you bring** us more coffee, please?
3. Ben can **drive**, but he prefers **to** take the bus.
4. A few of our classmates can't **come** to the school picnic.
5. **Could** / **Would** / **Will** / **Can** you take our picture, please?
6. Come in, come in! It's so cold outside. You **must be** freezing!
7. Jim would rather **have** Fridays off in the summer than a long vacation.
8. I must **read** several long books for my literature class.
9. Take your warm clothes with you. It **may** / **might** / snow. OR Maybe **it will** snow.
10. It's such a gorgeous day. Why **don't we** go to a park or the beach?

PRACTICE 29, p. 132

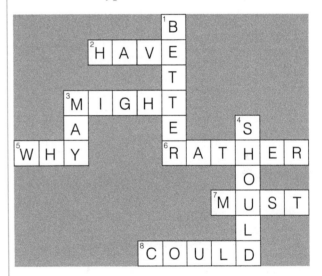

NOTES

NOTES

NOTES

NOTES

NOTES

NOTES

NOTES

NOTES

NOTES

NOTES

NOTES